My Mother's Daughter

H.J. Cummins

My Mother's Daughter

H.J. Cummins

Cathedral Hill Press

Saint Paul, Minnesota

Portions of chapter one were previously published in the Star Tribune.

Cover art by Jeremy Szopinski

Set in Adobe Jenson Pro 12/15

Cathedral Hill Press, 1043 Grand Ave #213, Saint Paul, MN 55105

Library of Congress Cataloging-in-Publication Data

Cummins, H. J.
 My mother's daughter / H.J. Cummins.
    p. cm.
 Includes bibliographical references (p.   ).
 ISBN 0-9742986-2-x (alk. paper)
 1. Cummins, H. J. 2. Journalists—United States—Biography. 3.
Cummins, H. J.—Family. 4. Cummings family. I. Title.

PN4874.C89A3 2005
070.92—dc22

                              2005027579

~: Contents :~

To Rosemarie, Barbara, Trisch and Leah

~: Acknowledgements :~

This was an audacious undertaking for me, and I want to thank the people who helped. My sisters, Barbara and Trisch, told me their memories of our shared past. Mom's favorite cousin, Gerhard Schneider, and his wife, Luitgard, in Germany, knew things I'd never heard before. My grandfather's memoir took me back an extra generation. Frau Ruth Wagner, of Dresden, generously shared stories of her life with me, a stranger to her at the beginning. The research team of The Minnesota Longitudinal Study of Parents and Children opened the world of attachment science to me. Dr. Eric Weitz, director of the Center for German and European Studies at the University of Minnesota, helped me understand wartime Germany. Drs. Klaus and Karin Grossmann, who pioneered attachment research in Germany, found time to talk to me about their work. Dr. Gerhard Suess, whom I may now call a friend, instructed me as to what I needed to learn while I was in Germany. Judy Hartford let me read the records of our counseling sessions in New York. Dr. Eric Johnson, my surgeon, gave me copies of my medical records. Ginger Rothé, my gifted editor, kept me going while I wrote it. On a more personal note, I want to thank my family in Seward, Nebraska—Aunt Jane and all the Jones cousins—for the love and care they always showed my parents. I also want to thank my mother, who turned out to be one of my most important teachers. And my daughter, Leah, who has brought such joy to my life that this writer is at a loss for words to express it.

❧ Introduction ☙

It was not until my mother's funeral that I found out her real name. I'd always thought it was Rosemarie Agnes Cummins. It wasn't. It was Agnes Rosemarie Cummins. She'd flipped the order when she emigrated from Germany after World War II.

How did I not know that?

Maybe she told me, but I wasn't listening. No, I decided, remembering all those times I had asked her to tell me about her life, about Hitler, or her mother who died, or the scar on the left side of her throat.

"Oh, I don't remember," she'd sometimes say. Or, "That was a long time ago. Why would you want to know about that?"

She dispatched me so quickly, I always felt I'd been wrong to ask.

When I look through the family photo albums, I see my young mother with happy, red-lipstick smiles, holding her babies and, later, posing with my sisters and me in our matching corduroy pants or polka-dot dresses or crocheted sweaters—all of which she had made for us. Yet the single strongest emotion that I remember from all those growing-up years was that she didn't like me.

She died of lung cancer when she was seventy-five, on September 26, 2000. In a second jolt of mortality, I spent much of that August and September in the hospital with a life-threatening illness of my own. It took me a long time after that to think of anything but death. And when I closed my eyes in prayer at church, it was always my mother's face—in old age, with silver hair and set jaw—that rose in the blackness.

By now, I knew more about the hard life she'd had. Three years before her death, while I helped her convalesce after hip surgery, she indulged my questions. Her answers became a six-hour, audiotaped account of a brutal father, a horrific war and a survivor's grit.

I had also reached some understanding of the hard feelings between my mother and me. There is a whole science around mother-child attachments. If they work as nature intended, they employ a caring, sensitive mother to prove that the world is a safe replacement for the cradling womb. For a baby, it's like having an all-powerful god on your side. At its best, this earliest relationship creates both security and confidence—like a mother bird gives both a safe nest and flying lessons to her babies.

But these attachments don't necessarily work as nature intended. Mothers are not always caring and sensitive—often because the world has not been such a safe place for them. To survive they learned to develop strength and toughness, and to amputate sensitivity.

It seemed clear to me that that is what happened to my mother. So I decided to go to Germany, to find out more about her hard life, the attachment research there, and what all of that could tell me about her, about me, and about our scratchy relationship.

∽: Chapter 1 :∽

My friend Gwen Krieser showed a photo of the old family homestead to her mother, dying in a nursing home last year in Lincoln, Nebraska. It was taken in 1943, with lots of relatives gathered around, on the farm near Waterville, Iowa.

It was one of those old, shiny black-and-whites with the sharply scalloped white edging. Gwen was always looking for something pleasant to bring her mother to help pass the long days. Her mother didn't remember the occasion of the photo, and showed no interest. But it set Gwen to thinking about providence and accommodation.

"Looking at that," she told me, "I was stunned to think what we have all been through since then: deaths, divorces, alcoholism, financial losses, disappointments. If some god had appeared on Grandpa Hager's carefully mowed lawn to pronounce our fates, we would all have been lying flat on our backs on the grass instead of smiling so confidently into the camera."

Mom was an unapologetic two-pack-a-day smoker most of her life. Ever the pragmatist, she did cut way back in my dad's last years, as his smoker's cough got worse. "Pretty soon we'll have to have an oxygen tank in here and then I won't be able to smoke, anyway," she told me.

But then after he died, she smoked more than ever. Mornings, she'd sit in her recliner quilting and smoking and watching TV and doing the newspaper crossword puzzle all at once. Because she used a pencil, she considered herself a dabbler. She had no problem erasing her first or second guesses. Still, she did so well it was easy to forget that English was her second language.

She was a morning person, so over the years when my phone would ring before eight in the morning I was pretty sure it was Mom. That's why the call early one summer morning in 2000 didn't alarm me until she said, "You better sit down."

She delivered the bad news fast: She'd gone in for a routine chest x-ray before her second hip replacement surgery and they saw a spot on one lung. She was going in for a CT scan today. The hip surgery was called off.

"Telling you girls this is the hardest thing I've ever done," she finished, and took a breath.

Then I sat down.

My words stumbled over my thoughts. They don't know what it is yet, right? So maybe it's cancer and maybe not? In any case, I said, one of us three girls would be with her for the next six weeks—time we had scheduled to care for her through the hip surgery convalescence. Now we'll deal with this instead.

She was sorry to be such a bother, she said, and that was the first of many times I wanted to cry for her sake. But I didn't cry then, and I didn't ever—if she could see me. Mom was especially impatient with tears. I never saw her cry in my whole life.

Now, home for my mother was the small town of Seward, in Nebraska. My little sister, Trisch, came from Phoenix to take the first two-week shift with Mom. Our older sister, Barb, came from Oklahoma City for the second. We stayed in close touch by phone. It took the entirety of their two stays for all the specialists to finish their diagnosis.

Some days were hard, like when Trisch called to say the fist-sized tumor led one of the techs to take her aside and caution her, "You girls should prepare yourselves for the worst."

But by the end of Barb's visit, the doctors were telling Mom that the chemotherapy and radiation treatment she chose could give her another four years of life, to seventy-nine.

I came from my home in Minneapolis just as the six-week course of chemotherapy and radiation treatment started. Her schedule of appointments and medications was so complicated I thought I might as well turn my many notes into a full-fledged journal. I am a newspaper reporter, and I asked Mom if it would be okay for me maybe to write about this episode in her life.

She looked at me with a slight smile and that powerful determination that always settled in her jaw. She wanted to be clear that she planned to claim those promised four years.

"Okay," she told me, "but your story has no ending."

"That's the good part," I said.

The plan was for my sisters and me to get her through the treatments and buy her those years. My journal was to record the process and the recovery we all hoped for. Instead, I would leave her, and my journal entries would end abruptly because of my own illness.

MONDAY, JULY 31, 2000

I see that Monet is big in the cancer world. Those water lilies of his are in every waiting room we sit in today.

This is Mom's first of three straight days of chemotherapy at an oncology clinic in nearby Lincoln. One round is now, the other in three weeks. Her six weeks of radiation are through a Lincoln hospital, eleven in the morning Monday through Friday for the next six weeks.

In the half-hour drive from Seward, I tell Mom that I hope she's not beating herself up about smoking. She's not, she says. She has always enjoyed smoking, it's the only thing she ever found that stimulates her and calms her at the same time. She knew the risks, she says, and I admire her for acknowledging that.

She will continue to smoke through all her treatments. No doctor ever asks her if she has quit.

Our first appointment is eight thirty in the morning at the oncology center. A nurse takes Mom into a treatment room with nine chairs, chemical-drip poles, and cabinets with pillows and blankets. The drip can be chilly, the nurse says. Then she asks Mom to choose from among the free chairs. I wonder if it's something they're trained to do, something that's supposed to subliminally give cancer patients the feeling they have some control over what's happening to them. Mom and I sit together through a two-hour drip of chemo drugs and an energizing antidote—a steroid.

I hear a young woman at the other end of the room. She looks to be in her twenties. She's clearly on the phone with her insurance company, talking about her liver and pancreatic cancer. She recites her call-back number, explaining that it's her sister's cell phone, which she borrows on her "chemo days."

There's also an older guy, his blue jeans held up around

his wide paunch by some bright red suspenders. He wears a billed cap over his bald head. He starts telling the nurse about how his dog keeps jumping up on his lap at home. At first he sounds cross, but an affection quickly takes over. The nurse listens.

We go to Perkins for a late breakfast, and Mom eats two scrambled eggs, two sausages and a slice of toast. This is the beginning of my obsession with logging every piece of food Mom eats every day. She is a big-boned woman, five foot eight inches tall, and only 122 pounds now. She is certain to lose more weight through the treatments, and that scares me.

For the next two weeks, we don't go anywhere without a satchel of medical files, x-rays, CT scans, and cancer publications. There's: *Radiation Therapy and You* and *Chemotherapy and You* and *Taking Time: Support for People with Cancer and the People Who Care About Them*.

At the hospital, Mom gets called to her radiology. While I wait, a skeleton of a man comes in and sits down beside me. "I keep wishing I'd be in the wrong place at the wrong time and take a bullet in my head, instead of dying slow for six years," he tells me.

He makes a joke about how he lost five pounds in one day—that was how much the tumor weighed. He has three children, and begins to recite their birthdays to me, except he forgets the youngest. He has memory problems, he says.

I don't even want to think of all the ways cancer may diminish my mother.

TUESDAY, AUGUST 1

Mom wakes up at three in the morning, and hearing her I get up. We know that it's because of the steroid, a painkiller and speed rolled into one drug.

Today the oncology appointment takes a strange turn, when Mom's doctor asks her what she has decided about surgery. My understanding is that she wasn't a candidate for surgery. Mom looks confused, too.

Mom's first expressed preference for treatment had been: "Do nothing." I thought the chemo/radiation had been her second choice, after the doctor told her that if she did nothing, he couldn't promise her even another two months.

"That was like signing my own death warrant and I'm not ready to do that," she had told me.

Now the doctor is saying that if she wants to consider surgery we'll have to stop the chemo now. Then, under anesthesia, there'd have to be some biopsies of lymph nodes between the lungs. If those are clear, the doctor could open her chest and try to remove the whole tumor plus a "margin" around it—a formidable task given its size. The surgery would be risky, blah, blah, blah. . . .

What's becoming obvious to me is that surgery is a bad option and that's why Mom didn't choose it. But somehow that wasn't clear in her records, which led to today's confusion and second-guessing.

After all that, we go ahead with the day's chemo. And radiation. Then, home again.

I'm already mapping out the four weeks of treatment facing Mom after I leave. My cousin Nancy volunteers to drive Mom to her treatments in Week 3. Mom and I will line up some of her friends to drive her in Week 4. Then I'll come back for Weeks 5 and 6. I'm trying to convince Mom to fly to Trisch's in Phoenix for a couple of weeks after her treatments end. Mom's not ready to think that far ahead.

WEDNESDAY, AUGUST 2 ·

Mom wakes up at three in the morning again. The steroid makes her feel "wired and tired at the same time," she says. This is the first morning that she dozes through part of the chemotherapy, her last of three doses until the end of the month.

She's so tired that today she will make some rare mistakes with her English. When someone asks how her treatment is going, she says, "I'm waiting for the other foot to drop." Another time she mentions something is "a bone of discontent" with her.

Today, like others to come, we talk about Dad, who had died almost eight years earlier of throat cancer. He was seventy-five.

They had met in Germany after World War II. Hal Cummins was a tall, skinny Army sergeant who'd suffered through most of his war duty in a German prisoner-of-war camp. Then he was one of the U.S. soldiers who stayed—or even returned, in his case—to be part of the Marshall Plan to rebuild Europe. Rosemarie Näther was a raven-haired secretary and translator in a series of U.S. Army offices. People who knew her then said she looked like Judy Garland.

Rosemarie was on her own, her mother dead and her father now in a Russian prison. Hal brought her cans of SPAM and olives. He endeared himself to her landlady by giving her some fresh onions. He was smart and funny, Mom said. And he was taller than she. That was her number one requirement.

They married in Frankfurt, and Rosemarie followed him to postings in Oklahoma, where Barbara and I were born, then Louisiana, where Patricia was born, and then Alaska, Kentucky and South Carolina, where he finished his twenty-year military career. In 1961, they moved with us three girls to Seward, where Hal had grown up and his family still lived.

Dad was a four-pack-a-day smoker. He was also an

alcoholic who quietly drank himself to sleep every night with beer and peach schnapps, until about the time I left home for college. He sobered up, after Mom finally threatened that he'd lose us otherwise. Then he retired from his job early, and switched his addiction to golf, which gave him great pleasure for years.

Now Mom is talking about his last months, when they'd take drives through the countryside and how he just loved to look at those Nebraska farm fields. I feel bad I'd forgotten that about him, about all the "pheasant hunting" we girls had done with Dad, when he never once reached for his shotgun.

THURSDAY, AUGUST 3
My journal is accumulating recipes, from all the food family and neighbors are bringing—a sweet noodle pudding is one, and there's apricot-glazed chicken and a corn casserole.

Mom and I both sleep until five in the morning. "Maybe this is a sign the steroid is wearing off and you'll start catching up on sleep," I suggest.

She's testy. "No. I had the sweats all night. That's a sign that the steroid is wearing off," she says. Then she jumps down my throat for buying too many Q-tips.

It's our first morning without chemotherapy, so we prepare leisurely for our trip into Lincoln. She's in and out of radiation in minutes, and then we drive back to Seward to see the family doctor, Van Vahle. Mom has known him for decades, because she'd been the receptionist at the Seward Clinic, where he practiced. He delivered my daughter, Leah, by now starting graduate school in social work at Catholic University in Washington, D.C. And he had cared for Dad until his death. That kind of continuity is rare in medicine these days.

Mom starts to fill him in, direct as ever. That it took the specialists five weeks from the time he'd found the spot in her lung to get her into treatment. And that when the doctors asked her first choice, she'd told them it was to do nothing. "Well, you know my sense of humor," she says.

She tells him she had felt fine the first three days of treatment, "and now I want to ask you to play God and tell me how I'm going to feel for the next six weeks."

So far, the only answers we've gotten are an evasive, "Well, everybody's different," from nurses and technicians, or the exhaustive lists of side effects in the cancer publications that scare us so much we stop reading.

Dr. Vahle gives Mom some idea of what to expect. "Radiation kind of beats you up," he says. And because it scatters, it may reach beyond the tumor into her lungs, and maybe her stomach. Mom might feel short of breath, and she may find that lots of small meals will be easier to digest. He recommends plenty of fortified drinks—instant breakfasts and pump-up formulas.

He tells Mom she doesn't have to deal with nausea. She has Compazine from the chemo doctors, but he can also give it to her in a shot if she needs it.

I can see that Mom feels better as we leave. I realize the word "cancer" was never spoken.

Mom sleeps from noon to one thirty and then four to five that afternoon. She would have gone to bed about seven, except her neighbor Cheryl pays a visit. She animates Mom with local news. They think one of the cooks was involved in that rash of thefts at the retirement home, she says. And they airlifted one person from a crash on I-80 west of Lincoln—one semi and three cars involved. "That's our turnoff to the hospital," Mom tells her. "We drove there just this morning."

I make Mom a chocolate instant breakfast as an afternoon snack and bulk it up with ice cream. She has some pan-fried potatoes and a dill pickle for supper. I try giving her a glass of wine to take the edge off her discomfort while she watches *Who Wants to Be a Millionaire?* Instead it nauseates her, so we retreat to Sprite.

About nine, Mom goes to the back deck to smoke. She had taken Extra Strength Tylenol, but it wasn't having any effect. She goes to bed, but gets up again about midnight with a hard pain in the right side of her back—about where the tumor should be, she says. She has me get a couple of shoeboxes of old medicine out of the hall closet, and she takes two pills from a 1998 prescription marked Acetaminophen #3. Within minutes, she's throwing that up, gagging into a hand towel. So we try more Compazine.

She's exhausted. "I knew it couldn't be that easy," she says, thinking back on those first few days. Her head drops forward to doze every few minutes, until the pain sticks her right side again and startles her upright.

We talk about Dad's cancer.

He had followed the oncologists' recommendation for radiation. The protocol delivers two years of life, on average. But my frail Dad was not average, and the treatments hit him hard, burning and blistering his neck. He never rebounded and died about a year later.

Mom thinks the problem was that he was just as burned inside, which made it hard for him to eat. "Or maybe he would have died that fast, anyway," she says. "Who knows?"

I tell Mom that I expect she faces the same hard time as Dad did, as the treatments assault the body, but that unlike him I really expect her to recover.

I hope it's okay to tell her that. I mean it to be encouraging.

What I don't say is that I think she's tougher and fiercer than he.

FRIDAY, AUGUST 4

It's another day of naps and pain. Mom calls Dr. Vahle at nine in the morning and gets prescriptions for a Compazine suppository and Ultram pills for pain. "Throw all your old pills down the toilet," he tells her. She does, and I'm surprised by her compliance.

At radiation she tells the technician, "Don't do anything that hurts. I had a rough night."

"That's not from the radiation," he says. I wonder if it's the chemo.

We've made an appointment to have Mom fitted for a wig this afternoon, but that's not for an hour. I suggest lunch at Burger King. We can eat in her car, more comfortable seating than in a restaurant.

She wants a malt and fries, but she sips the malt slowly and loses interest in the fries after just a couple.

"I'm pretty much going to be a bitch about you finishing that malt," I tell her.

She grins and says something like, "Oh yeah, like that's anything new," her voice carrying irony and love and humor, and we both laugh, happy that she can still be sassy.

Mom is so spent that she dozes in the hairdresser's chair. She picks out a wig that comes closest to her own short, no-fuss haircut. There are also catalogs of hairnets and hats and caps and scarves for people losing their hair to chemotherapy. The hairdresser suggests Mom buy a nightcap, because a lot of her customers say their bare heads get cold while they sleep. Mom picks a white one, with black lace.

I don't know if Mom ever wore her wig. I do know she liked knowing it was there if she wanted it.

At supper, she squirms with pain, still that right side. Mom says she has decided to try to get by on Extra Strength Tylenol during the day, and use the pain medicine only at night. "There's no honor in suffering," I tell her. Dr. Vahle said the same thing, I add, remembering his clout on the old-pills issue this morning.

She decides to take the pain pill. Only later does it occur to me that she's supposed to take just one a day, and I can't remember if she already had. I'm not doing well at keeping all this straight.

SATURDAY, AUGUST 5

Naps and pain, again.

And more of my notes on her eating: a third of a cinnamon roll for breakfast; cereal and a banana for lunch—most of the banana snuck under the table to her schnauzer, Sammi.

I think her body is functioning like that of an anorexic, that she really doesn't see how little she's eating. I also think the cigarettes sate her, in the way food would.

Trisch calls in the afternoon and asks about the wig fitting. "Mom opted for the green spiked look," I say into the phone, knowing that Mom can hear. She laughs.

Her friend Millie calls to see how she is and Mom learns that Millie has just had bladder surgery. They catch up on one another's medical conditions. Cheryl #1—next door—

stops by to say that Cheryl #2—down the block—has signed on to drive Mom to radiation one day in Week 4.

In the evening, Mom goes to watch the movie *Michael* on the TV in her room, so she can stretch out on the bed. I take a quilt and sit on the floor beside her. She reaches and takes my hand, saying, "This is so boring to you." I cry silently, because I can't remember my tough German mother ever holding my hand like that before.

SUNDAY, AUGUST 6
More naps and pain.

Mom wakes up at three in the morning, and smokes a cigarette on the back deck. Then exhaustion shoves her back to bed and sleep, until about six. Another third of a roll for breakfast.

When she sits, she babies the pain in her right side by putting all her weight on her left hip, the arthritic hip that was to have been replaced.

"The body's a funny thing," she said. "This hip hasn't spoken up lately. It's like all the pain moved to the other spot."

Her friend Norma becomes ride #3 for the open week. Norma works at the hospital, and she had come to see Mom the day the x-ray with the spot showed up.

"You saw my film?" Mom said, when she saw who was at the door.

"What are you going to do?" Norma asked.

"I don't know yet," Mom said.

"I'll help you sort it out," Norma offered.

Mom's friend Gladys signs on for ride #4. And another girlfriend Teddy calls to say if her leg problem goes away, she'll handle the fifth ride.

Longtime friendships are so precious.

Somebody in the family checks in every day. My cousin, Dave, and his wife, Jean, stop by before church. Mom is cheered. She tells us that she's happy family and friends went with her to all the doctors' visits, because she realizes she was in denial and doesn't remember half of what was said.

When it's just the two of us again, I ask her how long she was in denial. It's the kind of touchy-feely question Mom hates.

"I just thought I'd sail through this," she says, with finality.

Later I ask if she'd like to talk about moving into one of the apartments at the new retirement home north of town, when her treatments are finished.

"Not yet," she says, in the same tone.

It occurs to me that Mom chooses to grit this out one day at a time, as her hard early years had trained her to do. She spent most of the war in Czechoslovakia, working for a kind of a Nazi youth services agency, first in Prague and later in Budweis. Then, as the Russians came from the east, she walked or caught all manner of rides back, deep enough into Germany to reach American-held land. She had survived strafings and random attacks on railcars. She had slept in ditches or barns to avoid any Czechs, virulently angry over German atrocities. She went to sleep every night, silently pleading, *Please let me wake up tomorrow.* And she woke every day, pleading, *Please let me find one potato or one apple today.*

She willed her own survival then. It makes sense to approach this threat the same way.

I think that's what convinced my mother that emotions are of little consequence in life.

"If you stopped for feelings, you'd be dead," she told me.

MONDAY, AUGUST 7

We've been up most of the night because of the pain in Mom's side. She can't get comfortable any way she tries to sit. I see her fold over in pain, her hands on her knees and her head in her hands. In the morning, she takes some Tylenol and she's in and out of bed for a couple of hours. She is supposed to meet with her radiation doctor this morning, and we hope he'll have some answer for the pain in her side.

She can't bear the chairs there, so she stretches out on

the examination table while we wait. The nurse asks about her side: "On a scale of one to ten, how would you rate the pain?"

"Nine and a half," Mom answers. "It's not quite child-birth, but it's close."

The nurse introduces a new worry: The pain could be a kidney stone or a bladder infection.

When the doctor comes, he orders a CT scan, but Mom shakes her head. She's so fed up with tests. She gives me a look like, *Make them stop*, but I'm afraid the doctor might be right, so I don't. It's the first time Mom has ever asked me to protect her. She closes her eyes, and the only thing I can think to do is take her hand.

"I feel like a mouse lost in a maze with no idea what's coming," she says.

We go to the waiting room for the CT scan. The earliest she can get in is two hours away, and Mom's upset. "He just wants to use his fancy machine," Mom says. "He just wants to protect himself from any malpractice charges," I say.

I start checking out the wigs on women around the room. One is a kind of long, Sophia Loren look. Another is gray and tightly curled, with bangs a single tube across her forehead. A young woman's is short, sleek and blond. I look at Mom's hair, but I see no sign of it falling out. It is, in fact, a shiny gray and quite lovely. I had never really noticed that.

A young woman comes in for an appointment. In a touching show of support, her husband and daughter come along, wearing sunbonnets to match the one that hides her bald head.

Another young woman has her radiation "target" painted on her cheek and forehead. That means the tumor is in her head, and I take that as a bad sign. She sits with her family, silent and tired, thin except for a distended stomach. Her son—I'd guess he's about eight—keeps asking his dad, "Is Mom still sick? Is Mom really sick since she's not in the hospital anymore?"

"Stop asking stupid questions," she finally snaps.

Mom and I have our last fight about food, right there in the waiting room. Mom weighed in today at only 119 pounds. She lost three pounds in a week.

"You've got to eat more," I tell her. "You don't want to go through all this shit"—I motion around the hospital meaning radiation and chemotherapy and pain—"and then get in trouble because you didn't eat enough."

I'm pushing too hard, and she reasserts herself as my elder. "It's hard for me to think fondly of food right now. Look, I'll do the best I can and if that's not enough and I have to go in the hospital, then I'll go in the hospital."

The nurse comes to tell Mom that she's going to get her some pain medication. Mom, clearly touched by the care, says, "I'm sorry I'm giving you such a rough time."

"You're giving me a rough time, too," I poke at Mom, in mock anger.

"That's the power of blood," she tells me. Then she laughs: "Sometimes blood is *bad* blood!"

The humor gets us through the tense wait, and we start talking about us three girls—our various relationships with Dad, our marriages, our divorces, our children.

TUESDAY, AUGUST 8

I'm up about five thirty, and the dog wakes Mom about six. She slept through the night for the first time since treatments started, thanks to Ambien.

She's in good spirits. She eats two eggs and a slice of toast. She even takes a power bar, and eats it in the car coming home from radiation. It's such a relief to have only that, the one-minute treatment this morning, and no other doctors' visits or tests or hair appointments.

No CT scan results yet, the nurse tells us. She'll call if anything startling comes up.

We're home in about an hour.

I do some errands in the afternoon, and pick up a couple of shorts and blouses for Mom. Now she'll have something new to wear, for fun, and she looks happy. In some ways she is so easy to please. Any caring gesture touches her.

WEDNESDAY, AUGUST 9

Mom sleeps all night, again.

At the hospital, the doctor says there's no evidence of a kidney stone. He says the pain is too severe to be related to the radiation, so he makes an appointment for Mom with her oncologist for next Monday. She receives the news stretched out on the examining table. She's so small. Even her skin is too big for her, like a coat that needs taking in.

Later Mom tells me that the next time she has a pain, she'll just keep it to herself.

I notice something about the nurses and doctors in the radiation clinic. They let you talk. They don't interrupt you or cut you off. It sounds like a small thing, but it's not.

More than anything, Mom's exhausted. Everything takes hard effort. She sleeps during most of our daily drives to treatment. She naps much of each day.

"I'm pretty worthless these days," she tells me.

"You get total slack these six weeks, and you should take advantage of it," I tell her. "I may never be this nice to you again."

She picks up on the joke: "Yes, it's a rare pleasure to have daughters be so nice to their mothers."

"That's why I'm keeping a journal," I say, "so I'll have documentation."

Mom does complain about itching skin, which sends me back to the radiation and chemo booklets we have, to take another look at the possible side effects: fatigue, loss of appetite, skin burn, mouth sores, cough, fever, headaches, muscle and stomach pains, anemia, dizziness, diarrhea, infection, blood clots, confusion, depression.

Talk about depression, I can see why we stopped reading the discouraging list. Still, it reminds me of all that Mom's poor body is going through, and again her strength amazes me.

This is where my journal ends, as the days took on a sameness until I left, the next Monday.

I got sick three days after I got home to Minneapolis. I was up all night, throwing up. The next day the doctors diagnosed a small bowel obstruction, the result of scar tissue left from earlier surgeries, that twisted and finally blocked my intestines. My body's natural mending material had turned on me. The only treatment is more surgery, which of course makes more scarring, but there's really no choice. You just hope the new scars won't turn on you again. And the odds are more than eighty percent in your favor.

But this was already my second episode. The first blockage had happened just as suddenly four years earlier. Then, I'd had surgery to cut away the obstructive scars, and after three or four days my system kicked in again, and I went home.

I expected the same this time. My worry was Mom. This was Friday, August 18, and I had planned to go back to Seward the next Friday, to cover her last two weeks of treatments.

My bigger worry was my daughter, Leah, who was visiting me at the time. I had moved to Minneapolis from New York only after she'd gone off to college. And now, here she was in a strange town calling cabs to get her vomiting mother to the doctor's office and then the hospital. I hated giving her such a scare.

Doctors operated that evening. The surgical records noted "multiple adhesions" that took awhile to clear, and then the surgeon stitched me up. The final note was: "The patient tolerated it well and left the operating room in good condition."

Leah called my mother and my sisters, to tell them what was happening. The next day she had to fly to Washington, D.C., to start school.

I was sent to a room. A tube ran through my nose, down my throat and into my stomach. It would drain my stomach fluids into a jar hanging beside the bed, because even that bit of fluid cannot pass through a nonfunctioning intestine.

Thus began my obsessive monitoring of this jar. As long as muck continued to fill it, that meant my system was closed down. The end of muck was to be my signal of recovery.

I can't recount the passage of the next few weeks as accurately as I can my weeks with Mom. I kept no journal, at first because of fatigue and nausea, and that annoying tube. Then, as the days passed and I began to realize I was really in trouble, it was fear and inability to focus that stopped me from writing.

My intestines refused to open up. I remember getting wheeled to x-rays of my abdomen, looking for bubbles or bulges that could explain the continued clog. Even with the tube down my throat I vomited on the metal table, and the tech looked really disgusted.

I marked the passing days by the many roommates who came and went.

One was a young woman with adhesions from a sexually transmitted disease years earlier. She was hoping that they were the reason she was having trouble getting pregnant, and that surgery could fix things.

Then there was a woman who had an abdominal incision that got infected. She'd been a Medicaid patient somewhere else, and she suspected she hadn't gotten the kind of follow-up care better-paying patients do.

Another was an elderly woman who'd had a medical emergency at home, and now her children and a hospital social worker were trying to find some kind of care center where she could live.

One other old woman was taken quickly from the room one night. I think I overheard nurses saying that she had died.

One roommate was a beautiful, blond young mother who came in with her husband and their pastor. She'd had stomach cancer a few years ago, and now she had nausea and vomiting. It looked like the cancer had come back. "But I'm hoping I have what you have," she told me. A single room opened up and she took it, so her family could visit more easily.

I couldn't will my body to function, and the nurses said the only thing that might help was movement. So probably eight or ten times a day I'd pad up and down the hallways, pulling the stand with my drainage jar along. In one hallway hung a big print of a spring bouquet. I thought of Mom, because my assignment when I left her was to find something new to hang over her living room couch. It had been one of the many ways we'd expressed our optimism. "Let's buy some new things to enjoy when the treatments are over," we'd said.

I couldn't talk because of the tube down my throat. A friend, David Hanners, came every night. He was the person who stayed in touch with my family. Trisch and Barb each took a turn back with Mom, and he spoke with them and with Leah almost every day. There wasn't much to say, except that I seemed to be doing okay, and that I was walking every day.

Twice, the nurses pulled the tube out, thinking maybe they'd seen some improvement. Both times the vomiting started almost immediately. Then they'd have to put it back in, while I gagged.

Ten days passed. My condition was unchanged, except

that I'd lost about fifteen pounds. And I was getting more and more worried. I'd lie awake until four in the morning, pleading, *Please let me sleep*. I'd wake up, pleading, *Please let my body recover today*. A little like Mom, I guess.

On the tenth day, the surgeon talked to me about my lack of improvement. I wondered if the first operation hadn't cleared all the problem scars, and so did he. We decided on another operation, that evening.

The surgery took seven hours. The doctor told David that he'd started cutting with a scissors, but the scars were so hard and thick he had to go to a heavier scalpel. He had cut until he could massage a bubble of fluid through my entire intestines, as they lay outside my body. He said now we'd just have to wait. He also said it was a good thing I was so healthy in every other way, that a weaker person probably wouldn't have survived the surgery.

I think it was two or three the next morning when I came to, and David was there. The nurse asked, "Do you know where you are?" I said, "Burger King?" a lame joke to suggest how hungry I was by now. She looked alarmed, but David smiled.

I woke the next day, hopeful, partly because the doctor had also inserted a drainage tube into my stomach to replace the one down my throat. My first disappointment came fast, though, because the stomach tube didn't work, so they stuck the old kind down my throat again. I also had another new tube inserted near my heart that somehow fed me, so now I had two tube systems to roll along with me when I went walking.

Two of my best friends came to see me that day, unfortunate timing for them. They'd gone online to get me more information on adhesions, and in a lighthearted gesture, they included some articles speculating on a connection between human abdominal problems and aliens from outer space. They had no way of knowing how sick I was, or even that I'd had a second operation. Their good humor only reminded me that the world was going on just fine without me. I felt alone, afraid, and with absolutely no control over my predicament—three of the feelings I hate the most.

I went through a series of despondent thoughts, wondering if they were fair or overdramatic. It occurred to me that I was hooked to machines that were keeping me alive, so that essentially meant I was on life support.

Also, the throat tube continued to confound me. Fluid would stop filling the jar, so then nurses optimistically took out my tube. Then I'd vomit and they'd put it back in—always trying to say something hopeful while they did. After a while, I lost track of what was real hopeful and what was made-up hopeful. Once, about four in the morning as I headed into sleep, I remember thinking, "This is what it feels like to die. You've lost track of reality, your body has stopped, and you're not pulling off one of those great, spunky efforts to save the day."

Mom would occasionally call my hospital room, for a short, one-sided conversation because I couldn't talk, and I loved her gesture to stay connected. Most of the time, she sounded groggy and I assumed it was all the pain medicine. One day, Trisch said Mom had had her photograph her after all her hair had gone, with a shiny, bald head. "It's for my story that H.J.'s writing," she told her.

David struggled to know what to tell people about me, because there were no developments. I wasn't getting worse; I just wasn't getting better. So he relayed any detail he could think of. That I'd gotten some nice flowers that day from my boss. Or we'd taken a walk through the hallways together at night. Or he'd brought me a change of clothes.

I think that's why Leah was stunned by news of the second surgery. She felt she'd had no clue that I wasn't recovering. So far away, she now started to imagine the worst instead of the best.

I kept up with Mom's condition as much as I could, through what I suspect were shielded accounts from David. By now, I looked so full-time afraid and lonely that he wanted to tell me only good things.

Then, almost two weeks after the second surgery, my

intestines started to work. Unpredictably and painfully at first, but at last bile was coming out of the appropriate orifice. I was reluctant to trust in my recovery, especially because I threw up everything I ate for the next two days. But it didn't seem to worry the doctors, who sent me home on September 14—twenty-seven days after I'd gone into the hospital.

I threw up most of my food at home, too, for a while. I held off telling anyone, for fear I'd have to go back into the hospital. Then, gradually, the yogurt and chicken broth started to stay down. My throat was sore, but at least I could talk again.

Mom's last radiation treatment had been September 11.

I couldn't stop thinking about death. I obsessed over the news that an eighteen-year-old sailor on the USS Cole was killed in a terrorist bombing in Yemen. I tried to turn mortality into a question of math. Is it fair to die at eighteen? *No way*, I was sure. What about forty-nine—my age? *No, but lots of people do. That's probably the life expectancy in some countries*, I told myself. What about seventy-five—Mom's age? *Eighty would be better*, I decided.

On Friday, September 22, Mom asked to be checked into the local hospital. She was down to 106 pounds. Dr. Vahle put her on IVs of potassium and, I think, glucose. The next Monday, about four thirty in the morning, Mom couldn't catch her breath. Dr. Vahle tried a series of drugs to regulate her heartbeat and steady her breathing, with only limited success.

I talked to Mom on the phone that night. "I'm always out of breath," she said. "Well," I told her, "the doctors will have to figure that out for you."

Those were my last words to her, and I will always wonder if I said the right thing. I was still colluding with her expressed conviction that she would recover. Did she now want someone brave enough to talk to her about death?

Barb drove to Seward the next day to be with Mom. She got to the hospital just before noon. Mom was in a restless sleep, agitated and uncomfortable, waking to pull a sheet up one minute, then kick it off the next.

Dr. Vahle came to Mom's room to tell Barb the results of a new x-ray. Mom's heart was compromised, and the tumor was unfazed by all the treatments. Mom then became alert, and in a characteristic move that still makes me smile, she again asserted herself: "Van, you're mumbling. Come closer so I can hear you." He leaned to tell her, "I'm sorry, Rose, but the treatments didn't do what we'd hoped. I think we should start thinking about hospice arrangements."

It may just be a daughter's futile effort to comprehend death, but all three of us think that's the moment Mom decided to give up the fight. Over the next few hours, the bedside monitor showed her heartbeats spread farther and farther apart until they stopped. Her breaths followed.

My big sister was with her the whole while, telling her how much we loved her, and holding her hand.

Barb called me that night. It had fallen to her to carry out Mom's wishes to donate her eyes, and to be cremated. I got clearance from my surgeon the next day to fly, and went down to Seward the following day. Trisch came about the same time. It was good to be together. We laughed as much as we cried, telling Mom stories.

We buried her in a bright purple cloisonné urn, in honor of her love for exuberant color, next to our father, in a family plot north of Seward.

I came home for another month's recuperation. One day, David's pastor, Russell Rathbun, visited me. We'd never met. I remember my part of the conversation as basically: "Come in. Would you like some tea? What is the meaning of life? And excuse me while I cry through this entire conversation."

When he gave me his view on life after death, I realized it was the only answer I could have accepted. He said no one really knows for sure what happens when you die. But he finds life, basically, to be a good thing. So he figures that whatever the great force behind the universe has in store for us next, it will be basically good, too. I appreciate the logic in his answer. And it dodges uncertainty—something I handle badly. His answer is uncertainty, but not quite.

Over the next few weeks, I felt better. Each day my naps got shorter and my walks got longer. I spent some time looking for any possible way to avoid getting sick again. There is none. It may happen again, it may not. It is as simple and as hard as that. I keep checking with my surgeon, to see if medical science has found anything new. So far, nothing. I've gotten copies of my medical records. The notes after my last surgery say "re-exploration for a bowel obstruction would be a horrendous undertaking." I find it hard to believe I would survive another episode.

I try to think what Mom would say. What comes to mind is a story she told me about a woodpile falling on her neighbor's truck in Seward. Cheryl didn't know what to do, but Mom just got to work.

"You gotta start at the top," Mom told her.

"How do you know that?" Cheryl asked.

"I've dug people out of bomb shelters," Mom said. "You can't work any other way. You just have to start with the top rocks and work down until you're finished."

That was my mother's matter-of-fact way. You do what you have to do.

So about my illness I think she'd tell me, "Stop feeling sorry for yourself."

That's that gasp of hurt she could always give me.

She'd also say, "Stop thinking about it. There's nothing you can do about it, anyway."

And I think: *You're right, Mom. I'll try.*

~: Chapter 2 :~

Austrian-born Holocaust survivor Ruth Kluger, in her 2001 au-tobiographical "Still Alive," wrote that she grew up to be a not "overtly affectionate" mother. How could it be otherwise, raised by an emotionally detached mother in such a tragic time?

Once, as a very small girl, Kluger asked her mother, "Whom do you like better, my big brother or me?"

"I like him better because I have known him longer," Frau Kluger answered—a response both chillingly logical and per-fectly oblivious to the child's tender feelings.

And there was the night in Auschwitz when Kluger's mother came to her bunk and proposed that they die together by walking into the electric barbed wire around the camp. Frau Kluger is certainly not the first mother to wish a quick death over long suf-fering for her child. But in Ruth Kluger's young mind—she was twelve—the person God had created to protect her, the person who was supposed to dream of a daughter's beautiful future, had decided instead that she must die.

I started therapy with Judy Hartford on December 7, 1993. I was living in New York then.

In answer to the standard (I'm told) first question, "Why are you here now?" I answered:

My marriage ended two years ago. My father died a year ago. And my only child will go to college a year from now.

In other words, I was about to hit the trifecta of melancholia.

Judy recorded: "A feeling of sinking. Not going away."

In answer to the usual second question—"What was your family like, growing up?"—her notes show this answer:

My father was very critical, except at nights when he got drunk. I remember thinking, as a girl, *My own father has to be drunk to like me.* I was intimidated, in fact a little frightened, by my mother and her loud, commanding voice. My older sister was rebellious enough to keep my parents pretty busy, so mostly I tried not to add any problems. My younger sister seemed the most easy going, although she'd had a spell of ulcers in junior high school.

About a month later, just after New Year's, I walked into Judy's office with a fresh dream that I think delivered a metaphoric—or psychoanalytic—answer to why I was looking for therapy:

I am a reporter at a party with other reporters. It is outside, at night; white lights, wet pavement. I talk to a lot of people. I seem to know many of them. Then I realize I've lost my backpack so I start searching for it. I go into a building, downstairs, where there's a laundry room and a swimming pool full of dirty water, with college freshmen in goggles swimming laps. There are also dirty fish. The washing machines are spilling out dirty laundry, and they look irreparable.

The host sees me—I have the clear impression I shouldn't be down here, witnessing all this—and he ushers me back upstairs. I'm still looking for my backpack when I bump into an older woman who says her daughter told her to meet her here. I introduce myself, and she says she thinks her daughter has mentioned me. She starts to help me look for my backpack, but I resent it and I think, *How can she know where it is? It's futile.*

Then a guy I know from work finds my backpack, and he puts it on me. Now the scene of the party is changed to a bombed city, with flames of burning liquid. My friend from work and I go to another party. I spot a freshman woman defending her use of human subjects in research. At one point I hear her, self-assured, say to the host, "Yes, I used them but only because I found them for myself." I see her take aim to knock a person off a tightrope and I say to myself, *Her job is to figure out why this movie is called Birdland.*

The interpretation of some elements seems pretty clear to me now: the search for myself (my backpack), the stumble upon deep, hidden troubles (the dirty water), doubting an analyst's ability to help ("It's futile"), and being preoccupied with college freshmen (my daughter).

I'm also pretty sure I know what was behind the *Birdland* comment. It was a reference to a movie I'd just seen, *Waterland*, based on a novel by Graham Swift. It takes place in the marshy fens region of England, where the dampness all drains through a canal into the sea. A murder is exposed when the body gets caught in the dam at the end of that canal.

To me, the lesson of the dam is this: People can't escape their muck. They may try to hide it, but eventually it just clogs up the works. It was time for me to tend to my muck. And it's always best to start from the beginning.

Our family began on December 8, 1948, when Hal Cummins married Rosemarie Näther in Frankfurt, Germany. They met over a can of SPAM. My mother was working as an interpreter for the U.S. Army. My soldier father, who spent about the last nine months of the war starving in a POW camp in Poland, was part of the early recovery and reconstruction efforts there. The War Brides Act of World War II, which gave foreign brides an automatic pass to immigrate, was to expire soon. So Mom and Dad flew to the United States just after celebrating Christmas in Munich. Dad's first Army orders stateside were to join the motor pool at Fort Sill, Oklahoma. They moved to nearby Lawton, into a simple box of a house, with a crawl space below it and walls in need of another coat of white paint.

Mom was still starved in those early years. Dad remembered that she would bake a cake and eat every bit of it before it was even cool enough to frost.

While they were watching *Gone With the Wind* at a drive-in, Mom's water broke. Barbara was born November 17, 1949.

They named her after St. Barbara, the patroness of artillerymen, because Fort Sill was the home of the U.S. Army Field Artillery School.

I came along pretty quickly, on June 16, 1951. We moved that same year to New Orleans, where Dad taught ROTC at Tulane University. We were there for three years, and Patricia was born November 8, 1954.

Barb and I have only random memories of New Orleans. Screen doors up and down the block banging as kids ran in and out all day. Scooping up little frogs that would come out onto the streets in the daily rain showers.

Barb also remembers water tickling her eyelashes as she was pulled under by a whirlpool at Lake Pontchartrain. Before she felt any danger, a hand came down, grabbed her arm and pulled her up. It was Dad's.

His next assignment was Fort Richardson, outside of Anchorage, Alaska. We were there four years. It was a fun place for kids. We saw bears on the school playground on winter days. We built snow forts. And because we lived in base housing most of that time, we were surrounded by other young families and lots of playmates.

The photos from those days reveal Mom's youthful attention to fashion and beauty. We all had home perms. Mom made a lot of our clothes, but twice a year she'd order something for us from the Sears catalog. Because Barb and I were so close in age, Mom usually bought us variations on the same clothing. One summer we each got three sets of pedal pushers and shirts. Barb's clothes were always blue and mine were red, because she was blond and my hair was dark. That, apparently, was the color code of the time.

Dad often spent evenings working on his paint-by-number landscapes. This should have been an early clue to his exacting nature: He never dipped a brush in the jars of oil colors. He trusted only the fine point of a toothpick.

After he died, I found a brittle news clip from an Anchorage newspaper among the family albums. It's a five-paragraph story about a "quick-thinking" Fort Richardson sergeant who saved five-year-old Jeffrey Abbott from a charging cow moose by turning his car into the moose's path and then racing the engine to scare her.

The story ends: "Mrs. Abbott, who witnessed the near accident from an upstairs window, was unable to find out the sergeant's name, but expressed her thanks for his quick, thoughtful action. The child was unharmed."

There's nothing written on the clip to explain why my folks saved it. But there's no doubt in my mind that that sergeant was my dad.

My ear infections began when we moved to Alaska—I was three—and recurred throughout our four years there. Our trips to the base infirmary became a frequent occurrence. I remember hiding behind the living room couch when it came time to take my medicine, because the liquid penicillin tasted foul and Mom had no sympathy. I learned to swallow pills younger than anyone I know.

Mom's entries in my baby book show her impression of me then: "Harriet is a solemn child, very happy by herself. Smiles rarely, chuckles when she's happy." And: "Harriet had a hard time fitting into groups. She was sick a lot and missed a lot of school. She is so far definitely not an easy mixer, very sensitive." And: "Her temperament is emotional and she is very easily upset."

I take those notes, today, as signs of weakness by her measure. Another entry in my baby book supports me on that. My disappointed mother wrote: "At six, she is still too dependent on me, refuses to fix her own breakfast, etc."

Dad taught us to ice-skate when I was five. I remember the first time. We were outside and it was dark—like most of winter in Alaska. We girls sat in the snow beside a lit rink, while Dad tied up the laces to our new skates. I already knew that three pairs of ice skates were quite an extravagance for my family. I'm not sure how I knew that, because our folks never talked to us about money. Nor, honestly, did I ever doubt my parents would provide. But I knew we shopped very carefully at the Post Exchange. Potato chips were a rare splurge. I saw that Mom sometimes felt the need to defend the cartons of cigarettes she bought with an, "It's the only thing I do for myself" comment to no one in particular at the checkout.

One day, a neighbor down the block came to have coffee with Mom. She told us her husband was getting his Army discharge and they were going to start a horse ranch. I said I wished I could live on a horse ranch, and Mom suggested I go live with them. I thought maybe Mom was mad that I'd said something bad about us to someone else, or maybe she was making fun of me. She helped me pack my suitcase, she walked me down to the neighbor's and said, "Good-bye" and "Have fun." The neighbor lady told me that little girls in her house had to take naps, and she took me upstairs to their extra bedroom. I decided I'd rather go home and be ashamed than stay and be scared, so I got my suitcase and walked home. I went to my room and unpacked alone. Somehow Mom thought this was a funny story, and she always loved telling her friends about the time she helped me run away from home.

My only recurring dream started in Alaska:

I'm a little girl sitting on the pipe railing on the back porch of our base quarters. The witch from "Snow White"— pointed hat, hooked nose and chin wart—comes up the porch steps and offers me an apple. I take it, eat a bite, and tumble backward toward the ground, poisoned. While I fall, I tell myself, "That was stupid. How could you be so stupid?"

Dad's next orders were to Fort Campbell, Kentucky. We drove. My folks used to joke that we never needed vacations; we just moved a lot instead. It was 1959 and stretches of the Alaska-Canada Highway were still just mud. Dad built a platform over the floor space between the front and back seats in our brown '54 Chevy. Every morning my folks gave our terrier, Toby, some kind of sedative and put him underneath the platform to sleep all day. We three girls colored, cut out paper dolls, took naps and fought on the space above.

Thinking back, I don't know how we put up with all the cigarette smoke from my parents. I don't know how they put up with three little girls on such a long trip, either.

We rented a house just across the Kentucky border in Tennessee, but we were there only three months. There was a mix-up in the orders. The Army had sent Dad to an airborne unit and, as he said, "I'm not going to start jumping out of planes now."

So the next and final stop in his twenty-year Army career was Fort Jackson in Columbia, South Carolina.

We lived in a small, one-story house. We girls shared one room, which barely fit our single bed, double bed and two dressers. Another bedroom was our playroom, but we spent most of our time outside. We used fallen pine needles to mark off the many floor plans of our pretend houses—living room, kitchen, baby's room. We played family, and took turns being the husband and wife, being pretty fair about the roles as I remember. We pretended to smoke the seedpods from the catalpa trees, which looked like long cigars.

We walked to school with a load of other kids in the neighborhood. Barb and I basically did nothing for the first year there, because our Alaska school was that far ahead of this one. She remembers singing "Dixie" every morning instead of saying the Pledge of Allegiance. I remember being sent into the hallway as punishment, because somehow in the course of some lesson I referred to "The Civil War."

"Down here we say, 'The War Between the States,'" my teacher said. "You can sit by yourself for a while and think about that."

The civil rights movement was stirring things up during our time in the South, 1959 to 1961. Lunch counter sit-ins were happening in several states. Rosa Parks had held her bus seat in 1955 in Montgomery, Alabama, but most city buses in Columbia were still segregated. Barb and I remember the first time we ran to sit at the back of a bus, naturally drawn by that long back seat and wide window. People gaped and Mom had to tell us to come to a front seat. When Barb demanded an explanation, Mom found a way to make it sound polite: "Because if you don't, it will mean somebody else won't be able to sit down there," she said.

(After accommodating ourselves to Southern ways for three years, our move north to Nebraska was almost as traumatic. Barb remembers running to Mom in a panic, at the Miller & Paine's department store in Lincoln, because she couldn't find "the white people's bathroom.")

Mom's early life in Nazi Germany led to a puzzling combination of passion and indifference to political events. She got excited reading newspaper articles to us about Rosa Parks. She said, "This country could use more people like that." But other times she claimed no interest in history. "I learned it all wrong, and it's too late to change that now," she told us.

She had no interest in political parties. "I believed in one party once, and look where that got me," she said.

It was in South Carolina that I first remember being really afraid of my dad.

I don't remember the circumstances that launched one of his favorite sayings, but I know I started hearing it a lot. At the smallest transgression—running through the house, leaving a toy outside—his rebukes took one of two turns, and anything I said just made it worse. He asked me, "Did you know that was wrong?" If I said I did, he said, "Then why did you do it?" If I said I didn't, he gave me a hopeless scowl and said, "Well, you should have."

My worst memory happened during one of my many ear infections. One day, getting out of bed with the thermometer in my mouth, I dropped it. The glass broke and spilled mercury. Even hot with fever my greatest fear was Dad getting mad, but he surprised me by saying, "That's okay. Just pick up the pieces." I got on the floor and reached for a drop of mercury, but when I pinched it to lift it, it split into two. I tried again, and that drop split, too—as mercury would, I now know. I tried again and again, and more and tinier dots spread out in front of me. I remember thinking, *Dad tried to be nice and all I'm doing is making a mess.* I looked to the doorway hoping I had time to try to save myself. He was standing there, laughing at me.

Only later did it strike me: He thought it was funny to scare a sick child.

Those were the days before vaccinations. Over our Alaska and South Carolina years, Mom nursed us through mumps and measles and chicken pox, their contagion usually making our illnesses concurrent or quickly consecutive—an exhausting proposition to a mother. This was about the time of the polio epidemic, too. It's easy to forget that not so long ago, even for middle-class mothers in the United States, seeing their children through 103-degree fevers and life-threatening complications was no small part of their responsibilities.

I appreciate now how certain I was that Mom would always take care of us. But anything like cuddling or commiserating was not her style.

One day at school a bee stung me in my mouth. I hadn't noticed it when I bit into my apple during morning recess. I knew I was more frightened than hurt, but I still wanted to go home. The nurse called my mom, and she came and walked me home. She told me I needed to get over letting stupid things like this upset me.

Another afternoon I came home to find blood on the living room floor and all over the bathroom. Normally Mom and Trisch would be there, but I couldn't find them. I don't remember exactly what I did—maybe I went in my room and closed the door?—but eventually they came home. Trisch had stepped on the sharp rim of the coffee can where we kept our crayons, and Mom had to get a neighbor with a car to drive them to the base infirmary. I told her I'd been afraid something horrible had happened, like a killer came to the house.

"Oh, don't be silly," she said, fed up with my high drama.

I worried about the whole family, not just me. Like the time in second grade that I rode along to the telephone company office with Mom. She applied for a job as a night operator. I sat on a wooden bench in a waiting room, and I watched Mom talk to a man in his glass office. She didn't get the job. The man said he wouldn't hire "Army wives" because they always move away, she told me on the way home. She said that wasn't fair. I knew she was upset, or she would never have spoken about such an adult thing with me.

After three years in Columbia, my dad got his discharge papers. He was happy to leave the Army. He'd earned a pension. If he'd stayed in, he would have been sent to Korea. Also, at Sergeant First Class he had probably seen his last promotion. The Army gave him two shots at Officer Candidate School, but he blew them both by being drunk, Mom told us years later.

Besides, he wanted to get back to his beloved Seward, his hometown. Barb was eleven, I was nine and a half and Trisch was six. Dad got a job at the Conoco station on Highway 15, and for our first year and a half we lived in a big, old farmhouse three miles west of town.

Shortly after we got there, my folks went out one night. It was the first time, that I remember. I looked at it as one of the many changes to come in our new life. A cousin came to stay with us. She said she wasn't scared, because she lived out in the country, too. But this was 1961, only two years after Charlie Starkweather was executed for killing eleven people—starting in Lincoln, just twenty miles to the east. Now it was hard to get baby-sitters to agree to go outside of town, she said. Her story gave new excitement to the tree branches that would scrape my bedroom window some nights, swung by wind or weighted by snow.

On the farm we ran across cow pastures and invented secret spy clubs under the evergreens in the shelterbelts. Barb, who'd always been really thin, decided she'd become an Olympic athlete. She learned how to do chin-ups and started eating more, and she saw that it made Mom happy.

I think we all liked to see Mom happy, because she was our stability. Barb remembers once when Mom planned to go shopping in Lincoln with Aunt Jane. She'd bought a dress, a black-and-white mini-checkered shirtwaist. "It's fun to have a new dress," Mom told Barb. The day of the shopping trip, though, Barb woke up sick. She tried to hide it so Mom could still have her day out. But Mom saw, and canceled.

"I realized then that you give up a lot to be a mom," Barb remembers.

As soon as we moved there, Dad's drinking started to become a problem. He made his own beer in big crockery in the basement, and I could see Mom wasn't happy. One afternoon I awoke from a nap on the playroom couch and heard my parents arguing in the kitchen. It scared me and I didn't want to embarrass them, so I pretended to still be asleep. I heard Dad say something like, "I don't know what you mean," and Mom said, "Do I have to spell it out for you?" Then he left.

Mom had a miscarriage when I was in fifth grade. Dad took care of us. He said, "Your Mom had a baby, and it died, and so she has to rest." She stayed in their bedroom with the door closed, except when Dad went in with cups of black coffee and came out with balled-up bits of laundry. I passed much of the time on the couch in the parlor, next to their room. I found the idea of a dead baby upsetting, and it was also scary to go two whole days and nights without seeing Mom. I worked myself into a state, worrying that if a baby could die, then maybe Mom would, too. Barb's reaction was the opposite: Mom can handle anything. She'll live forever.

I think it was on the third day that she emerged. She started into the daily routine as if nothing had happened.

Soon after that my folks bought their first home. It was a small, cottage-style house in Seward, and we moved on my eleventh birthday. I remember because Mom was so busy she took me out to the front porch and handed me—one year late—a booklet from Kotex called "Now You Are Ten." She told me to read it, and went back to moving. It was a brightly written and simply illustrated introduction to menstruation. Somehow it didn't occur to my mother that a girl might be alarmed to learn she should plan on regular bleeding episodes for the rest of her life.

In the house in town, the rooms were small, but there were enough of them to give each of us girls a room of our own. I loved it. I finally started to read, after years of preferring to run around outside. The only book I read on my own before that was *Heidi*, which Mom made me read because it had been a present from my grandfather in Germany. Now, the first book I picked up was *A Tale of Two Cities*, although I have no clue why. Maybe it was part of a display at the city library.

Barbara, Trisch and I made more friends, because we could get around on our bicycles. We also joined in Seward's summer tradition of kids hanging out at the city pool. Some of the girls my age were already talking about boys, and meeting them nights at the Rivoli movie theater downtown. The pool also provided my sisters and me with our first jobs. The Red Cross Junior Lifesaving course was offered at age twelve. We each took it and started teaching swimming lessons right after.

Sometimes we bicycled to school, or Dad dropped us off on his way to work. I was in the seventh grade when, just after lunch in Mrs. Rediger's English class, someone from the principal's office came around saying that President Kennedy had been shot. A second knock brought news the President had died. This was deep into the Cold War. We had all had school drills teaching us to crouch under our desks or to walk single file into the hallway "in the event of a nuclear attack"—that's how they always said it. And although I don't think I ever saw a real bomb shelter, I'd seen pictures of them in Life magazine. When I looked at the scared faces of our teachers that day—November 22, 1963—I assumed they thought the Russians were coming.

That was a Friday. My family sat in the basement and watched TV news all weekend. In our house that meant CBS with Walter Cronkite. My parents knew we were watching history, and my dad took politics and world events very seriously. He talked to us about Lyndon Johnson, and said he admired Johnson's strong stand for integration. I thought school would be called off because of the funeral on Monday, but it wasn't.

After we moved into town, Dad got a new job as Veterans Service Officer for Seward County. He worked for the draft board, and also helped veterans with all their benefits. He had an office in the county courthouse, and I was proud of him.

One Saturday morning a farmer came to our house with some fresh-killed chickens to thank Dad for driving someone in his family to the VA Hospital in Lincoln. "I was just doing my job," Dad told him, embarrassed.

It was at times like this I most loved my dad—when he followed his strong, basic values and then was bashful about it. Like with Jeffrey Abbott and the cow moose. Like wanting us to feel confident about Lyndon Johnson. I'm pretty sure this drive to Lincoln was above and beyond his duties. Perversely, what made his anger so hard on me was feeling that I had disappointed a man who, at least in some ways, had such clear goodness.

Mom went to work, as a receptionist at the Seward Clinic. Everyone has to see a doctor sometime, so Mom met everyone. She gradually changed from an outsider in a small town to the ultimate insider. She knew more people than Dad. She talked to everyone. She loved it.

"Some people call it being nosy. I call it being curious," she said.

Soon after Mom started at the clinic, she told me, "You need a new winter coat." So we went to the Stylecraft dress shop downtown, and I tried on a brown wool coat with big black buttons down the front and a slim black collar—very Jackie Kennedy looking.

"Is this the one you like?" Mom asked, watching me in the mirror. I told her I did. I kind of expected her to size it up and then sew one like it for me, but instead she said, "Then we'll take it." She reached inside her purse, pulled out what must have been some of her first earnings, and she bought me that wonderful coat.

It was also about now that my sisters and I realized Mom had a German accent. We had just thought she sounded

66

like everyone else. I heard it for the first time when I called home long distance from a summer music camp in Lawrence, Kansas, the summer after eighth grade. Trisch saw some of her friends mimicking Mom—greeting them at the clinic—and she thought, "They sound like Colonel Klink on *Hogan's Heroes*."

Mom worked Saturday mornings, so Dad cleaned the house. Trisch picked up on how unusual it was in those days and thought it was cool. "God knows it was probably because Mom didn't do it right," she said, later.

I have some great memories of Dad during this time.

He opened a checking account for each of us at the Cattle Bank, and he taught us how to balance our monthly statements. When we weren't in school, he'd sometimes let us join in his regular morning coffee group at the Corner Café. I could tell these were the important men in town—the county treasurer, the bank president and the owner of the dry cleaning company—and Dad was one of them.

He pulled some funny pranks, too. When I turned sixteen and applied for my first driver's license, the tester marked every answer on my written test wrong. I was mortified, but gratefully he didn't leave me in suspense for long. "Nah," he fessed up. "They're all right. Your dad put me up to this."

Dad was nearly impossible to buy gifts for. He just never wanted a lot. Besides, he was so tall and thin—six foot two inches and 140 pounds—that regular clothes didn't fit him. So Mom mostly took over for us on Christmas and birthdays. She bought clothes for him at Jack Graff's, the best store in town and one that could accommodate special fittings.

"Just don't ever tell your dad how much these things cost," she warned us.

Every morning Dad plugged in the coffee percolator, which Mom had set up the night before, and got the Lincoln Star from the front porch. He read it every day and Time magazine every week. I'm sure this had something to do with my becoming a journalist.

He was amazing to watch at cards. He and Mom played bridge with another couple every Saturday night. He wasn't one for conversation while a game was on. He rarely looked up from the card table. He remembered every card that had been played, and he figured out where most of the rest were. If Vic hadn't put the ace of diamonds on Dad's jack, that had to mean Gladys was holding it.

But these were his darkest years—my junior high and senior high years—when it came to drinking. Every night after supper he went to the basement and turned on the TV. Then he drank himself into a stupor with beer that he kept in the basement refrigerator and peach schnapps that he hid in the garage. Mom always sat across from him in the TV room, knitting or hemming or working crossword puzzles. I think she didn't want us girls to feel responsible for taking care of him. And she worried about him falling up the steps at the end of the night.

His drinking meant we could never have friends over in the evenings, except occasionally in high school after a Friday night football or basketball game, because by then Dad was in bed.

In the midst of this, Mom had to go to Germany for a couple weeks to help her dad. That's when Trisch developed an ulcer.

"That clearly had to do with Mom being gone," Trisch says. "I wasn't happy when she was gone. Dad would drink. It was a time I realized how much she protected me. She really did keep things level for me."

Barb remembers Mom as "incredibly strong" and "managing everything."

Our dad could be harsh by day—"scathing" and "ridiculing" are some of Barb's words.

Barb and Dad had huge fights, mostly about her social life. She was pretty and popular, and she was out late a lot of nights in high school. Dad came down on her for slacking off on her house chores. And Barb was brave enough to talk back. I never was. I think it all reminded Mom of her fights with her dad.

I thought then that my job was to not add to the tension. I tried my best to be perfect. I spent a lot of time in my room. I studied a lot. I liked school and got good grades. I joined a lot of activities in high school—band, school newspaper, student council, pep club.

But eventually all of that backfired in a horrible incident with Mom. I was in the school literary club, and one night that the club was to meet I was sick. Mom told me to stay home. I said, "But I can't. I promised I'd be there." She looked at me really fed up and said, "Just who do you think you are?" As in, "The Queen of England?" As in, "Someone important?" I think I knew even then that what she meant was I shouldn't take myself so seriously, that I shouldn't push myself so hard. But those words sliced through to my soul, because top on the list of things that my parents hated were people who thought they were "big shots."

All the serious fights I would later have with my parents—why I wanted to go to graduate school, why I wanted to take a new and better job—were some variation on their theme, "Who do you think you are? A big shot?"

One day, my last year in high school, Mom woke Trisch and me—Barb was gone at college. She said out loud for the first time that Dad was an alcoholic, that early that morning she'd told him he had to stop drinking or she'd have him committed for treatment. Then she said, "Go tell your dad that you love him." She went into the kitchen and we walked into the living room, where Dad was sitting on the edge of a chair. When he looked up, I saw his sad and panicked eyes. We did tell him we loved him. He swallowed down tears to say, "Thank you." I think we went right back upstairs to our rooms, partly because we didn't know what else to do and partly because we got the impression that he just didn't want anybody looking at him right then.

Thirty-two years later, after Mom died, I found a note folded into her jewelry box. It was the pledge my dad wrote her that morning, October 6, 1968: "I request that my wife, Rosemarie, commit me to a hospital if I ever touch one drop of alcohol. Hal Cummins."

For a while after Dad stopped drinking, he gobbled cookies from the scratched-up Tupperware container on top of the refrigerator that Mom kept stocked. He favored sandwich cookies and anything with marshmallow. Mom said the sweetness helps against alcohol cravings. He finally put on some weight, too, with a new fullness around his middle and in his cheeks. And with very rare exceptions, he stayed sober the rest of his life.

Trisch has lots of happy memories from her high school years. She had friends over to watch TV so much Dad teased that he'd have to get rid of the couch and bring in bleachers.

It was my turn to become the problem child. I was at the University of Nebraska, in Lincoln. In the spring of my freshman year—on May 4, 1970—four students were killed during a protest against the Vietnam War at Kent

State University in Ohio. I joined the demonstrations on our campus, which included taking over the ROTC building. Dad, of course, was furious. I came home one weekend in overalls—clothing then associated with hippies and war protesters—and Dad was so mad he walked out of the living room without speaking to me.

I dropped out of college for a semester in my junior year, and took my grandfather up on his offer to pay for any one of us girls to come visit him in Germany. I worried that my parents wouldn't like it because I sensed they didn't get along with Opa. But I thought, how can I not go on this adventure? And I wanted to find out more about all my mother had left behind. My parents were dead set against the trip—but not because of Opa. Their objection, again, was the "big shot" problem. "You just want to go so you can brag you traveled all over Europe," Mom accused me.

This flap probably contributed to my Dad's view of me as "hopeless." Years later Trisch told me that the first time I invited a guy home from college, Dad called a meeting with Mom and her to say, "We have to do all we can to make a good impression. This could be her last chance to get married." I was twenty-one.

I did marry, and went away to Florida and New York to work on newspapers. My daughter, Leah, was born on March 12, 1976. Visits home were always nice because we'd all learned to avoid some subjects—politics and work, especially—and concentrate on easier ones—golf and TV shows and updates on all the grandchildren.

Mom and Dad were pretty happy empty nesters. Dad decided to try chickens, and he built a coop on my cousin's farm. The littler cousins loved helping Uncle Hal. They even had "Chickens Inc." t-shirts printed.

"That coop is better insulated than our house," Mom scolded. She persuaded Dad that they would enjoy a new place and they bought half a duplex across town, brand new. Mom loved it.

Barb, who lived closest and went back the most, said Dad grew almost effusive in his later years. "I know he loved all of us. And he practically waxed poetic about Mom, how special she was. I think that was the real him. He had just been fighting his own demons."

Trisch remembers the time Mom came home from a trip to Germany. Dad bought a "Welcome Home" balloon—and tied it to a skillet.

"That's as sweet as it gets with Hal," Trisch said.

Mom once told me she came to understand this about Dad: "Hal is hard on people. But he has always been hardest on himself."

Dad was diagnosed with throat cancer early in 1992. He died in January the next year, at seventy-five. The year he was sick Barb, Trisch and I tried to make sure one of us came home each month. Those were some of the happiest visits. It really is true that at these times small things stop mattering. There was a truce in the thermostat war between Mom and Dad. We took country drives and Dad talked about his favorite horse when he was a boy. He gathered his war medals—a Purple Heart, a Bronze Star—for his two grandsons.

After he died, I found out that he'd set up a "car account" at the bank for Mom. He calculated that she'd need one more car in her lifetime and he wanted to take care of that. That's when I finally understood my parents' love and care for one another. I thought, *Of course. This says "love" from Dad. Now I get it.*

Mom picked a Buick Regal, dark green. She said the color would look nice in funeral processions. At her age, it seemed like a reasonable consideration.

She asked me to help her figure out her finances. Dad had handled all the money for them, and I was the likely daughter to ask because I was writing a personal finance column in New York at the time. Her affairs were simple— Social Security, a paid-off house and some investments. I advised her, for tax and benefits reasons, to keep the investments but to sign the house over to Barb, Trisch and me. She gave me one of her hard stares and said, "Are you sure all this is fair to your sisters?" What she imagined, I have no clue.

It crossed my mind that maybe we finance writers, with all our warnings about scams, had made older people *too* suspicious, and this was my payback. But it also felt like an accusation taking us back into that painful "big shot" territory. Mom and I went to see my cousin, Dave, a banker.

We gathered in a bank conference room, with Mom's papers. Dave was very close to my parents, and they'd gone to him with money questions before. I repeated my advice to Mom, and Dave agreed with me. Now, she gave him one of her hard stares and said, "But what if I go through all the other money and I need the money that's in my house?"

It was the first time I'd heard her express that worry, and I wanted to answer her. I said: "Mom, if you go through all the other money and you need the house, it is there for you. And if you go through all the money in the house and you need more, we will give you more. We will take care of you."

Then I watched the most amazing thing. I saw a calm spread slowly down my mother's face—from the furrowed hairline, across her eyes and mouth, and finally relaxing the hard set of that powerful jaw.

Her suspicions were not mean or even unfair, I saw. They were the reasonable response to a hard life of personal and global betrayal. Life had taught her not to assume that anyone would take care of her.

She seemed to enjoy her last eight to ten years. I admired her openness to new things. She liked the reality show *Big Brother*. She had a crush on Dr. Kevin Fitzgerald on *The Emergency Vets*, on Animal Planet. The last movie she put on the "to-see" list I found in her calendar, after she died, was *Run Lola Run*.

Looking back, I realize there had been signs of Mom's care issues all along. Like the time three years earlier, when she needed to have her first hip replacement. My sisters and I arranged, then, too, to cover her six-week convalescence in two-week shifts. Before the surgery she saw a friend of mine downtown and told her, "My girls are going to come home to take care of me. It's so nice to have girls who take care of their mother." My friend said what struck her was a kind of surprised tone in Mom's voice.

~: Chapter 3 :~

Late on September 11, 1944, two hundred bombers dumped destruction on the target Darmstadt. Fourteen-year-old Ludger Heinz and his family passed the night safely in the basement of their home, on the edge of town. The next day Heinz hiked over smoldering mountains of debris to find his grandmother, uncle and aunt—planning to come to their rescue just like one of the heroes in his adventure books. When he got to their house, it was gone. One look at the blackened rubble and the still-burning basement, and he had no doubt that they were dead. Standing there, he inhaled the smell of their burning bodies, a smell like smoked meat.

All around him, he began to see that what looked like piles of burning coal were corpses, the remains of people who had been going about their lives just the day before. Some lay like small, compact bodies, some hung as particles of ash in the air. He couldn't cry a single tear. "We had become tearless," Heinz said, "actually physically tearless. Crying is supposed to bring relief, and there was no reason to expect relief."

— Kriegskinder, Hilke Lorenz, 2003
(Translated by H.J. Cummins)

After my mother's hip-replacement surgery in the summer of 1997, she was practically chair-bound. We made a deal: As long as I kept bringing her coffee and emptying her ashtray, she would answer questions about her life. Over several days, I discovered so much about my mother. I learned that she wanted to be a dentist or maybe a banker when she grew up. I learned she had a German fiancé killed in World War II. And I learned just how strong and tough my mother had to be to survive that war. Memories going back fifty years can be dodgy, and unfortunately she had forgotten a lot. Mom and I laughed often, as she talked about her stubborn streak, her Aunt Toni's cooking, and an embarrassing incident involving my grandfather—Opa—and an outhouse. After Mom died, I used those six hours of tapes, a one hundred-page memoir by her father, and a three-month trip to Germany to assemble a biography of Agnes Rosemarie Näther Cummins.

Agnes Rosemarie was born to Otto and Else Näther on November 11, 1924, in Halle, Germany, a small city midway between Berlin and Bavaria. It was just eleven months after an older sister had died in childbirth, something my Opa blamed on the midwife. My mother grew up an only child.

The families on both sides were country people, living in the German state of Saxony, a little north and west of Leipzig. The land around was flat, good for farming, and then climbed south and east to the Erzgebirge mountains around Dresden.

Three generations of men in Opa's family were welders and locksmiths, down to his father, after whom he was named. The elder Otto traveled for work when he was a young man, building distilleries to make potato vodka for the lords whose manors still dominated the German countryside. When he settled in Zschepplin and started a family, he brought the first bicycle to town. A socialist, he was also the first person in town to join a metal workers union—an act that provoked the lord there to rescind the family's use of his meadow for their own few animals and vegetable garden. They had to move, and they would move several more times over the years as Otto took a series of jobs in foundries and factories.

On Rosemarie's mother's side, Else Schneider's family owned a big, prosperous farm by Klitzschmar. One measure of her parents' wealth, according to the standards of the day: They had one team of horses and two of oxen. The compound of heavy stucco buildings included their residence, the barn, and a small inn and tavern. Travelers stayed there, and locals came for dinners and dances.

Mom already looked like her grown-up self in a baby photo shortly before she was a year old. Those are her dark eyes and round mouth. Sitting on a wicker chair, in a mackintosh-style winter coat with light chenille trim, she's holding a twig in her left hand—probably given to her to keep her still.

These were terrible times for Germany. Its people and economy were exhausted and in defeat after World War I ended in 1918. Hunger and cold killed thousands even after the war. Influenza took two thousand people in Berlin in just one day. Germany's war debt and iffy politics led to the hyperinflation of 1923 that devastated ordinary workers. A loaf of bread that cost twenty thousand marks one morning cost five million marks that night. A lifetime of savings now bought one streetcar ticket. Political extremists plied the general feelings of desperation to build followings. The most extreme were Hitler's fascist National Socialists—the Nazis—and the Communist Party.

Mom's young life was full of health problems. She was born with both feet folded up to her shins, so she spent her first nine months in a series of casts to force them down. She was anemic. She had rheumatic fever at five and jaundice at six—she caught her reflection in a mirror and called to her mother: "What's wrong with me? My eyes are yellow." As she grew, her left shoulder cramped high and close to her neck. So when she was seven, the doctors clipped a tendon to release it, this time putting her in a cast from her head to waist. Maybe because of all that, or because they had buried one child, her parents hovered with health tonics. They gave her daily doses of cod liver oil for a while, having to pin her on the floor and force it down her. About the third time she "accidentally" knocked the bottle off the windowsill and broke it, they gave up. "I was pretty strong-willed," Mom told me, laughing. "I just hated being manhandled."

As far back as she could remember, her favorite place was the Klitzschmar farm. Else's oldest brother, Otto, and his wife, Toni, ran it by the time Rosemarie visited. They were her beloved Onkel Otto and Tante Toni. They had two sons, Gerhard, a year younger than Mom, and Heinz, three years younger. Gerhard was her favorite cousin, and she was "the daughter Toni never had," Mom said. She dug potatoes during harvest, threw table scraps to the chickens, and requested a meal of beef tongue every slaughtering day. There are photos of Mom, very young, with Gerhard and Heinz bathing in a tin tub in the sunny farmyard. Others show them riding in a sleigh pulled by two white goats, and in a bigger, fancier horse-drawn carriage. Klitzschmar was also important to Mom's family because it kept them from hunger in hard times. Besides that, as a teacher, Opa's pay sometimes came in the form of meat and grain.

Opa's participation at the farm was limited because a World War I injury had shattered his right knee, leaving that leg shorter and unable to bend. When Otto Schneider inherited the family farm, as the first-born son, it was his duty to pay his sisters and brothers their share of its value. Opa spent all of Else's money on his university education and books. When Mom found out, she felt that was unfair to her mother. She objected to his higher education for another reason—it essentially locked her in her room every night until she was ten years old. Opa attended the University of Halle while he taught full time at an elementary school. His schedule meant that he taught mornings, attended university classes afternoons, and did his teaching preparations and university assignments in the evenings. For all those years he demanded that Mom be in bed and silent by seven at night, so she would not disturb him.

Those two clashed over and over. Mom defied Opa at school—an astute choice because intellectual success was everything to him. His memoir, unencumbered by modesty, frequently describes his genius. After his first year at his village school, where the teacher was "old-fashioned and stupid" and the other students inferior, he was sent to live with an aunt in Eilenberg so he could attend a proper city school. My take on his childhood is that his academic success mattered so much to him because he wasn't well liked by the other boys. He wrote that one time, when a group of them were catching crabs, the other boys laughed at him for crying after a crab pinched him. Another bad sign: Opa was always picked to play the female role in school plays.

From the beginning, Mom ran away from school. She neglected her homework. One day, bored with a teacher, she just walked out. Opa punished her for "willfulness, obstinacy and indifference." When she told me about this, she called them "spankings." But Opa's kind of spankings would qualify these days for a visit from Child Protective Services.

Mom adored her mother. In photos, Else has an oval face, dark hair pulled loosely back, and a smile like a crescent moon. I don't see her resemblance in Mom, or any of us girls. If anything, Mom took after her father, with a wider face and more dramatic features. The young Opa in the photos—shiny, bald head; round eyeglasses and always a double-breasted suit—looks just like the Opa I knew forty years later, less a lifetime of wrinkles.

I always wondered where Else was in this father-daughter duel. It seems that Opa's rules reigned. If Mom ran home from school, Else walked her back. Curiously, Opa doesn't write much about his wife in his memoir. Even Mom didn't tell a lot of stories about her. So I'm left to conjecture. And looking now at her photos, it strikes me she was probably a quiet person, a listener and abider—just what Mom needed.

The family moved often. Mom didn't like it and she blamed Opa's ambition—always scanning for promotions even if it meant going to a new school. But there were things she didn't know. According to Opa's memoir, after he got his Ph.D. from the University of Halle in 1934, he was set to become headmaster of a middle school in the nearby city of Weissenfels. But Adolf Hitler had taken control of the German government the year before, and Opa was not a member of the Nazi Party. So he was given the humbler assignment of fourth-grade teacher in the much-smaller Mühlberg. The next year, the University of Dortmund offered him a position as lecturer, but again the party stepped in and sent him off instead to a small middle school in Mückenberg.

My Opa had a generous portion of pride—not always an appealing trait. But to his credit he was never one to feel sorry for himself—not in times of war or hunger or even prison. Only once in his memoir does he complain, which makes it all the more heartbreaking when he does. Those insulting job assignments, he wrote, "destroyed all my hopes for the future and made senseless all my efforts that I had applied to my studies."

Finally Opa joined the Nazi Party. This is how he explained it in his memoir: "I was ashamed of myself, but what was I to do? The situation was such that one could either be for or against the system. Were you against it, you had to expect to be put on ice, to lose your job and eventually to be imprisoned. If you were for it, you had to show your readiness for cooperation. There was no alternative, at least in my job. If I wanted to survive, I had to submit and to accommodate myself."

Opa's passage raises the giant question of ordinary

Germans' complicity in Nazi atrocities. My grandfather clearly knew the party was doing something awful, or he wouldn't have held out so long. Maybe he and others struck a devil's bargain: Ignore signs of evil in exchange for the pride and profit that a conquering Nazi army brought home. When Opa and I talked about the war, I could never pin him down on how much he knew and when he knew it.

In 1938, Opa moved the family to Bad Liebenwerda, a small town known for its spa with curative, iron-rich mud baths. Opa's parents had built a big house there. The plan was for Opa to take a teaching job in the town's middle school and they'd all live together. But both parents were old and frail, and died about the time Opa, Else and Mom came. So their young family took over the main floor, and one of Opa's sisters, Mom's Tante Anna, took the upstairs. Mom remembered her parents modernizing the house with electricity and plumbing.

At thirteen, Mom was quick to make friends in her new town. They called her *Schwartze Rose*—"black Rose"—for her coal-black hair. She was tall, the kid in school photos who always stands in the middle of the back row. One of her best friends was Annelies, so small that her nickname was *Mücke*, or "Mosquito." Mom took the innocent risks of childhood. One day, she and some friends decided to swim across the Elster River by Bad Liebenwerda. The current took them far downstream, and they had a long walk home. They got back late, and Else, always afraid of water, was beside herself with worry.

Mom and her friend Ursula collaborated on a brief attempt to write a great love story. "We knew everything about books and nothing about love," Mom remembered six decades later. She spent a lot of time at her friend Opal's house. Opal's mother, a widow, was one of the few parents who indulged the children running in and out of the house during this time of coal rationing.

German girls started in Hitler's *Bund deutscher Mädels* (BDM) when they were ten. The boys had their own group, the *Hitler Jugend*. Meetings were held on Saturday mornings, which brought an end to the six-day school week, something Mom and her friends loved. At least at the beginning, these groups were much like Girl Scouts and Boy Scouts, Mom said. There were songbooks. There were crafts and games and parades and camping trips. They marched as a drum and fife corps, with Mom one of the drummers. It was all small stuff, she said, especially in the countryside, which didn't have the huge, charismatic gatherings that Hitler celebrated and filmed in the big cities. Still, every group activity was suffused with the ideology of Aryan supremacy, and there's nothing like starting young to shape minds. "Well, I think we were probably always extolling the virtues of the *Führer*," she said. "I probably believed everything they told me. I think I was a deeply convinced Nazi. I really was. And I do admit, I had to work very hard to overcome my anti-Semitism."

She knew families in Bad Liebenwerda whose handicapped children had been taken away, and who were later told that they had died. She knew some families whose politically active fathers were in concentration camps. But neither registered as ominous to her. "I wasn't suspicious. I was naive," she said.

She was fifteen when Germany went to war. She was outside in her yard, when Opa relayed radio reports that Hitler had invaded Poland—September 1, 1939. "I thought, 'Yay, you know, that was great,'" Mom remembered. She saw it as liberating the country, not invading it. After all, every European wanted to be German—"That's what we were told"—she said. She was now an officer in the BDM, and one of her duties was to bicycle around to homes and teach young girls to knit. Later, during the war, BDM members worked at munitions factories and wrote letters to German soldiers on the front, urging them to keep up their fighting spirit.

Also at fifteen, Mom started a clerical apprenticeship at an office supplies wholesaler in Bad Liebenwerda—a common vocation for girls in those days. As was the custom, she continued to live at home. The work didn't suit her lively style any more than school had, but the training qualified her for jobs later when she needed to work—right after the war, with the U.S. Army, and when we moved to Seward, at the clinic.

Opa still had a fierce temper. One family story recounts the time Mom's flamboyant and lovable Tante Toni Michaelis came to dinner with red polish on her fingernails. Opa all but called her a whore. "I will not sit at a table with the likes of that," he swore and left. When Mom was sixteen, he punished her for dating a boy whose father was a Communist.

"The last time my dad beat up on me—I mean really beat up on me—was when he found out I was dating that guy's son," Mom told me. "He was worried about his reputation, that his job could have been in jeopardy. That was the first time I confronted my dad. I said, 'You're lucky you don't have a son, because if I was a son I would hit you back.'"

Her personal war was at home: "I wasn't rebelling against the Third Reich, but I was rebelling against my dad," she said.

She happily left home for *Arbeitsdienst*, a year of public service required of young Germans. They took over the jobs left vacant by men away fighting the war. Mom's first assignment was to help with the wheat harvest in fields near the Czech border. Later, she sorted seeds into packets at a garden nursery. She also spent some time at a butcher shop, where she scrubbed horse blood off the butcher's block with lye.

Back in Bad Liebenwerda, she became engaged to a guy in her circle of friends, Klaus Buschendorf. His father was a Nazi officer. Their dates were outings with their friends—sledding, cross-country skiing, and going to movies in the town theater. When I asked her what the attraction was, she laughed and said, "He was tall." It was only a matter of time until he was called to fight. Toward the end of the war, the family got word that he died after a wounded leg was amputated. Mom never made up her mind if he was the victim of a used-up medical system—by now painkillers, disinfectants, and bandages were scarce—or if he just decided he'd rather die than live with crutches. "He was a very physical young man, very sporty, and I don't know that he would have ever been happy like that," she said. After all, he'd been raised to believe that handicaps were unacceptable to a "master race."

Did she ever wonder what her life would have been like if Klaus had returned?

"Oh, he would have made a terrible husband!" she said, laughing but offering no elaboration. If life had kept her in Germany, she figured she would have taken a secure kind of job, maybe in a bank, probably in a small town. "I would have put in my hours at work and then enjoyed my recreation time," she told me. "I would have been happy there, too."

Mom still didn't want to be at home. So she applied to a Nazi youth program in Prague, a party effort to win the hearts of young Czechs. She was hired as a music director, because she could play piano, recorder and a little violin. She said she enjoyed the work and the city, but it's hard to imagine a more hostile place for a young German. The Czechs had good reason to hate their occupiers. While Mom was there, Hitler destroyed the entire nearby town of Lidice. The Nazis suspected some connection between Lidice and an assassin of the German leader of Czechoslovakia, Reinhard Heydrich—hit by a grenade in May of 1942. So with gruesome cruelty meant as an example, German soldiers marched into the town of about four hundred, killed all the men and sent all the women and children to concentration camps. The soldiers even killed the dogs. Then they wiped the village off the map—the buildings, the gardens, even the graveyards.

Atrocities like this made Czechoslovakia a particularly dangerous place for retreating Germans after the war. A friend of ours in Bavaria remembered one bloody retaliation: On an arbored highway that crossed the Czech-German border by her town of Hohenberg, Czech partisans killed every German soldier they found and hung them, one to a tree, a horrifying spectacle for passers-by.

From Prague, Mom got home occasionally. She traveled by train, the cars by now infested with insects. After every trip, she undressed over a full tub of water to catch the bed bugs she'd picked up.

Her parents noticed a hoarseness in her voice. She thought it was just more of their overprotectiveness. But she did have her tonsils out and a deviated septum fixed in Prague—both with only a local anesthesia. "That's not real successful into bones, and it hurt like hell," Mom said of the nose work. "The surgeon was a Czech woman, and I kept trying to bat her away."

From Prague she was transferred to Budweis in southern Czechoslovakia, near the Austrian border. Again, she directed music programs. It was here she was nearly killed by a bomb. In air raids, planes are spaced to span the target width, and they fly several rows deep so that after the first line of planes drops all its bombs the second line starts in to cover the next stretch and so on. One day, over Budweis, one plane was a split second slow and left a thin rib of standing buildings. The apartment house to the left and the apartment house to the right of Mom's building were destroyed and the people in them killed. Hers was in that rib, unhit.

She never doubted that Germany would win the war. She wouldn't dare. Anyone heard questioning a Nazi victory was guilty of "defeatism," and could be sent to a concentration camp. But she also saw no reason. "We never had any defeats, you know, we only had 'strategic withdrawals,'" Mom said. Hitler promised a *Wunderwaffe* up to the very end—a miracle weapon so awesome that all their enemies would promptly surrender.

Because of his age and stiff leg, Opa was spared conscription. He stayed to teach in Bad Liebenwerda where his duties were expanded to include directing the Nazi government's social service programs locally. One of his stories, I think, demonstrates the horrible temptations that come with power. He wrote of a young man who wasn't working although he had a family to support. Opa decided that man needed to learn the value of work—a lesson Opa was now in a position to teach him. So Opa found him a job in a sawmill and told him to show up faithfully, or else. "Though in reality I hated the National Socialist terror, in this case it seemed to me the right way to underscore our goodwill was with a mild threat," Opa wrote in his memoir.

About this time, my mother's favorite cousin was drafted. Gerhard was just seventeen, but in their last gasp of fighting the Nazis were taking boys even younger. He was artillery, his group sent to Poland with six horses and one cannon. He saw immediately the war was lost, because all the veteran soldiers were deserting and retreating west. Only the new boys who didn't know they were beat stayed and fought. Gerhard followed the older soldiers; he was among those captured before they reached home and sent to a POW camp.

The worst of the war didn't come to Bad Liebenwerda until the very end. Situated on the eastern side of Germany, it was invaded first by caravans of refugees running from Russian soldiers, and then by the soldiers themselves. Fleeing families left behind their sick and dying, and most of their young men were conscripted on the spot if they ran into any German soldiers.

The Soviet troops reached Bad Liebenwerda on April 27, 1945—one day before Else's fiftieth birthday. The dark night brought mass suicides. A father killed his wife and daughter, then himself. A couple poisoned their four-year-old son and then themselves—only at the last minute the mother couldn't go through with it. There were seventeen dead by morning, in a village of about three hundred. They chose death over the violence they expected from the Soviet soldiers, who were raping, killing and stealing as they advanced west through German towns. And the soldiers lived up to their reputation in Bad Liebenwerda. The parents of a seventeen-year-old girl were killed trying to stop her rape. Mom's friend Annelies—*Mücke*—saw a Russian soldier slit her mother's throat. It was only luck that she survived; the hasty soldier held the knife backward—blade side out. Opa, Else, and Tante Anna tried to hide in the house basement, but they were found. The soldiers took Opa away. A frantic Else, certain that her Nazi husband was about to be executed, ran up three stories to the attic and threw herself out the window to her death. The soldiers took Tante Anna to an outbuilding where they beat and raped her. Mom believed she never really recovered, because a few years later Anna killed herself by walking into the Elster River. She couldn't swim.

The family had a hard time finding a minister to bury Else. The clergy worried even that gesture of sympathy would compromise their families. Only the Catholic priest was willing.

Opa and about forty other men were locked in a barn for two weeks and then released—partly because there was so much work to be done and partly because there was so much confusion as the local Communists competed with the invading Russians for authority. Opa was assigned to shovel coal in the furnace at the sawmill. He moved back into the Näther home, but now he shared it with at least three other families. He was arrested again in December 1946 after an English-language Reader's Digest was found in his room. That was just a pretense so they could take the house, Opa said. After a year in prison in Halle, the Communists offered to release him if he spied for them. He agreed, but when he got out he escaped across to the American-held part of Germany.

Mom spent the final days of the war making her way back to Germany—knowing nothing of the events in Bad Liebenwerda. She left Budweis on the advice of a tailor there, who sewed her a skirt and jacket with some black-market fabric Tante Toni had sent her. When he gave her the finished suit, he said, "Young lady, I want to tell you that the Czechs are going to rise up and you should get out of the country." She started south, planning to go through Austria. A German transport troop picked her up. They had already included another young woman, Hilda, and her two small daughters. Hilda's husband was an SS officer, still fighting or maybe dead, she didn't know. U.S. planes strafed their caravan; their suitcases were shot through. Somewhere in Austria, they ran into U.S. soldiers heading east. The Americans took the German soldiers as prisoners and let the others go. The Americans said, "The war is over," and Mom, facing enemy guns and tanks, stood firm in her disbelief: "That can't be," she challenged them.

No Austrians wanted to help retreating Germans, even women and children. They did help themselves to all the suitcases, though, which cost Mom her new suit. "No one had anything. I didn't blame them for that," she told me. Finally her little group of four found a barn where they stayed until another caravan came through, this one German farm families fleeing from Poland. One of their drivers had died along the way, so the families asked if Mom or Hilda could handle a team of horses. "Sure, I can," Mom volunteered. "I really had no idea," she told me later. "I had watched it on the farm, but I'd never done it." Soon her English skills were more valuable, anyway, as the group had to talk their way through U.S. checkpoints now set up along the highways. The women and girls left the caravan at Coburg, in northern Bavaria. They found a German army warehouse, with some sacks of rice and a tired collection of German soldiers, former POWs, trying to get back home. One of them said to Mom, "I know you from somewhere." It turned out he was one of the assistants who held her down during her nose surgery. "I guess I made an impression on him," Mom told me, laughing.

She was hospitalized in Coburg for typhoid fever. It was an American-run hospital, and by the time she was well she'd been hired as a translator. That was the winter of 1945-46. Mail was random at best. In November, Mom got a birthday letter from her Tante Toni reporting all the developments "after your mother died." It was the first Mom knew of Else's death; an earlier letter from Opa hadn't found her. Now she went back to Bad Liebenwerda, hiding mostly in railroad freight cars. If she were caught, she could not have come back west. On the way, she found her Onkel Otto and Tante Toni in Halle trying to make a living raising beaver for pelts. The Communists had taken the Klitzschmar farm. What silliness, Onkel Otto told her.

The party took everything in the name of the people and divided it evenly among six farm laborers. What to do with cow #7? They just shot it, he said. Mom found that another uncle had died of cancer; just days before his death his family shielded him from the news that his only son had been killed in the war. Cousin Gerhard had been liberated from a POW camp in Czechoslovakia. He found some old clothes and a rake and, looking like a farm boy, walked the ten-day trip home unchallenged. The hunger now was worse than during the war. Desperate mothers let their babies suck on fingers dipped in honey. It didn't nourish them; it just stopped their crying. Other mothers boiled veal bones and served the thin broth to their babies.

When Mom got to Bad Liebenwerda, Opa was working at the sawmill. He now had only one room in their house. He offered Mom the attic, but she couldn't imagine sleeping there after her mother's suicide. Opa also told her the Russian soldiers had defecated in their piano. "I guess the house must have been in pretty bad shape. I couldn't bring myself to go back in it," she said. So she went to a cousin's. Opa wanted her to stay in Bad Liebenwerda with him. Predictably, they fought. "I can stop you," Opa told her. "You know, I hate to remind you, but I'm twenty-one," Mom countered. "There is nothing for me here, and if you had any sense you'd leave, too." But he still hoped to get the house back.

Mom escaped one last time into the Allied-held part of Germany. She went to work again as a translator and secretary, in Amberg, also in Bavaria. The Americans were nice to the Germans, she said. One boss shorted two fifty-blanket lots one blanket each, and gave her both of them so she could sew herself a coat.

It was also in Amberg that she met my dad, in the summer of 1946. He'd come to the war through Normandy about a month after D-Day. He was captured not far from the coast and spent the rest of the war in a POW camp in Küstrin, now part of Poland. Later he joked that they passed the time there "lying to each other," telling tall tales they were pretty sure no one could ever check. "And we had a deck of cards. We played a lot of cards," he said.

Dad is famous in the family for the funny letter he wrote his mother after his capture. He started it: "Due to circumstances beyond my control, I've had a change of address."

He told a wartime story that, in its way, is deeply sad. After the POW camp was liberated, the American soldiers made their way to Odessa, on the Black Sea, where an Italian ship would take them to Naples. One night in Odessa, while an American movie played in the background, Dad looked out a window at two GIs, cooking a bit of scrounged food over a campfire. He heard a small rumble, then he watched one side of a building collapse on them. One died immediately; the other was still breathing when Dad reached him, but only for a few minutes. "I've often thought, god, you go through all that damn mess and you get clear down here and you have a wall fall on you," Dad said.

He was shipped home to the States to regain his health and strength. Then he re-enlisted, returned to Germany, and met Rosemarie. "I went back and got captured again," he always said—a joke my mother got to hear for the next forty-five years. Opa was out of prison and came to their wedding in Frankfurt on December 8, 1948. Opa told Mom he wanted her to marry a game warden, live in a forest somewhere in Germany, and he'd live with them. "He had it all figured out," she said. "That sounds really terrible now; that's the way things were done more or less in Germany then." She had another reason to want to go far away. "Just being around him in Frankfurt, I would get these awful rashes," she said. "He just brought out the worst in me."

As I talked to Mom about the war, one of the hardest things for me to grasp was how she could still care about ordinary things in such extraordinary times. How could she be preoccupied with dating while Nazi Germany marched across Europe, I pressed her? How could she possibly care about a fashionable skirt and jacket? Finally, the same kind of stories from other survivors helped me understand that of course people live lives on many levels simultaneously. In a German film documentary, one of Hitler's secretaries spoke of her own shock when she found herself counting her typing errors in his final dictation—only a couple through the whole document. In Ruth Kluger's story, she remembered her mother's fits when she learned her husband was having an affair in a refugee camp in France, after he'd been taken from their home in Vienna. His infidelity could be every bit as devastating to her as genocide.

In my trip to Germany, I had the good fortune to meet Frau Ruth Wagner, through a mutual friend, in Dresden. Over coffee and cake many afternoons, Frau Wagner was willing to share her family story with me. Now eighty-one, she was slightly plump, favored colorful sweaters and scarves, and wore her dark gray hair cut short and curled in a permanent. Her age showed in the deliberate effort it took to sit and stand from the café chair, but her conversation was always animated.

Born in 1922, Frau Wagner was two years older than my mother, so they grew up pretty much in the same time and place in history. She also felt a connection to America, because two of her uncles and aunts had immigrated to Milwaukee during the hard years before World War II. All four married spouses they met there who had also come from Dresden—through one of the many *Vereins*, or associations, that German immigrants set up to share memories and connections to their faraway hometowns. Frau Wagner had always hoped to visit her relatives in Milwaukee, but that travel was stopped first by the war and then the closed border around Communist East Germany. By the time she was free to go, she said, she was too old.

When we talked about Mom, we found many similarities in the two women's lives. Both grew up in small towns—Frau Wagner's was on the outskirts of Dresden. Both were leaders in the BDM. Both trained to do office work with clerical apprenticeships. Both lost many friends in the war. Frau Wagner said only four of the fifteen boys in her school class survived. And both lost fiancés in much the same way. Frau Wagner's shot and killed himself after an explosion destroyed both his legs, fighting in Salerno, Italy.

The fundamental difference, however, was that unlike my mom Frau Wagner was openly full of emotion. Her eyes still teared when she talked about the war, especially the firebombing of Dresden on February 13, 1945. It was Mardi Gras night, she said, so city pubs and restaurants were full of people celebrating. The waves of planes dropped bombs that collapsed most of the city's great baroque buildings and ignited fires so fast and so big that they instantly consumed all the oxygen. When Frau Wagner walked into the city the next day, she saw people still sitting straight up in streetcars, looking alive and on their way somewhere. The air pressure had exploded their lungs and left the rest of their bodies frozen in position, she said. Some bombs dropped phosphorous on the citizenry, coating their clothes, their skin and even their hair with fire. Efforts to wash off the burning chemical by running into the Elbe River were futile. Frau Wagner said she had to hide under a bridge to avoid second-day strafings from new rounds of English and American planes. Historians estimate somewhere between thirty-five thousand and one hundred thirty-five thousand Germans were killed in the bombing of Dresden, just three months before the war ended in Europe.

Despite such horrors, Frau Wagner thinks it was Opa's harshness even more than the war that trained my mother to drain events of their emotions. There was in Germany a very old-school philosophy that beatings were the best way to discipline children—and if that failed, humiliation would certainly do the trick. Opa sounds like one of the last true believers, Frau Wagner told me. Her parents never hit her. And when she studied to be a teacher after the war, she was taught that the two best ways to reach a child are praise and your own good example. I told her about Mom's rash around Opa. "Oh, that's hard," she sympathized.

Frau Wagner remembers great deprivations after the war. Her part of the country recovered slowly. She married, and she and her husband got a government permit to salvage bricks from the piles of rubble, scrape them clean and reuse them to build their house in a Dresden suburb—the house where she, now a widow, still lives. Her daughter sat in a baby carriage while Frau Wagner and her husband clawed their way to their allotted twenty thousand bricks, finding corpses and body parts as they did. Only the love and support of their families get people through such times, she said. She could imagine my mother feeling so alone in America. The alcohol added another burden, she said, but even if my father had been the best man in the world, he couldn't have understood what Mom had been through— no one could who hadn't lived it.

"Your mother had to be all locked up inside herself," Frau Wagner said.

In *Kriegskinder*—"Children of War"—German author Hilke Lorenz wrote about scores of Germans who were children during World War II. They all had the same basic memories of their early years: Survival left no time for tears. And the bar on sadness got raised to the stratosphere: How could you feel sorry for yourself when everyone around you was in such bad shape, too? If you whined about hunger, someone would say to you, "You're lucky, you still have both your parents." Or if you cried that your father was killed, someone would say, "Be thankful you have your mother. There are plenty of orphans around."

Those are exactly my mother's views. Her words, on the tapes:

"Basically, when you don't know where you're going to sleep the night, you don't worry about feelings. When you don't know what you're going to eat tomorrow, you don't analyze your feelings." And when I raised her mother's death, prefacing it with, "Now I know you don't like to talk about emotions very much, but …" she stopped me: "Well, I don't think I had any. Emotions are not a big thing. Emotions just do not come into play, because everybody's in the same boat."

What I love about this part of the tape is we both break out laughing. Mom got straight to this big difference between us, only this time we decided to laugh instead of fight. In the old days I would have said, "I can't imagine you had no feelings," and she would have said, "You have too much time to imagine." Somehow we dropped the reflexive assumption that we had to agree or else one of us was wrong. Somehow we were ready to do this. Which is why, I think, she felt she could continue her point without having to brace for me to challenge her: "I had to be a survivor, and some really weren't. I think that's part of getting out of scrapes … being a survivor. I think that's a gift, the fact that someone can rid themselves of some baggage and say, 'This is done. I can do nothing more about it. I have to look ahead.' And I pity the people who can't do that."

That day, as a grown daughter who loved and admired her mother, I understood her position. I didn't completely understand its effects on me as a little girl, though, until my trip to Germany when Gerhard's wife, Luitgard, told me a story from the first time she met Mom: I was in high school,

I had a boyfriend, and I was so happy when he brought me flowers. "So of course," Mom told Luitgard, "I had to warn her, 'Don't get too excited. Don't get carried away. You'll only be disappointed.'" I barely remembered that time, but hearing it from Mom's point of view just knocked me over. I realized that all those growing-up years, when I wanted her to be happy for me and wish good things for me, she was thinking: *I've got to toughen that girl up. I've got to get through to her what a dangerous place this world is, or she's not going to make it.*

Mom lived her credo to the end. When she got sick, my sisters and I had the impression that she would not even consider the possibility she might not make it. I think she was—protectively—less than candid with her daughters. After she died, her friend and former boss at the Seward Clinic, Dr. Paul Hoff, told us that he had stopped by the hospital to see her the day before she died. She was too breathless and weak to talk much, so he filled the visit with news about a family trip. Then Mom told him, "I just have one more trip. It's the one we all have to take."

And I think: *That's Mom, unblinking, no baggage:* "This is done. I can do nothing more about it. I have to look ahead."

~: Chapter 4 :~

In the tapes of Mom's memories, I asked her about Hitler: "Were you ever angry that this lunatic had ruined your life and so many people you loved had died?"

This was her answer: "I guess I had no emotions. You keep trying that feely stuff, but I just didn't. I wasn't angry. It was something that happened. Oh well, war is war."

I fell in love with my daughter when she was four months old. Until then, she was a tiny package of fear and failure, because I had no idea what I was supposed to be doing with her. She had colic, and cried hours every day. I was certain her pain was building to a dark shadow over the rest of her life. And it was my fault. And I felt stupid. And I hated feeling stupid.

Then one night, about midnight, I was trying to stop Leah's crying while I warmed her bottle. I looked at her, really looked at her: doe-brown eyes, fair skin, and soft hair the color of rust. I realized that in my mind I'd pictured me in a fight with this dear creature, in a rope pull and we were dug in on opposite sides of a line. At that moment, I mentally crossed that line to her side. I said my thought out loud to my baby, "It's not you against me. It's you and me against the colic."

I'd like to say that in this magic moment she stopped crying and I stopped fretting, but that's not real life. Leah stayed colicky a few more months. But those middle-of-the-night feedings were changed. They were sweet and close and the first time I trusted myself to take care of my daughter. I may be the only mother in history who looked forward to waking up at night to feed the baby.

I was twenty-five when Leah was born, fairly young by today's standards. It was the late seventies, the height of feminism. I'd graduated college Phi Beta Kappa, gone off to

Germany for a three-month break, and my then-husband and I had taken jobs running the weekly Seward County Independent in Nebraska. It was to be the first step in my journalism career. I soon learned I was pregnant, and I was happy about it. My announced conviction through the pregnancy, "This isn't going to change anything," sounds preposterous now, but I have since heard the same from many, many first-time mothers.

When I told Mom I was pregnant, she said, "Your first is always special." I thought it was an odd thing to say to her second child.

I expected to take a few months off, enjoy relaxing with the baby, and then jump back into work, refreshed by the pause. Then motherhood buried me in self-doubt. How can this be so hard, I wondered? Women have been doing this forever. I was embarrassed when my feminist friends came around. I felt like Exhibit A for anyone wanting to argue that women really can't "have it all." I let down the sisterhood. I was even more troubled by my apparent failure to effortlessly outperform my mother. I was so sure that I would naturally be more patient, more sensitive, more empathetic. I think maybe the only thing I was, was more scared. Still, I rejected Mom's advice to me then: "Just love your children and they'll be okay," she said. *No they won't,* defiantly leapt to my mind. *You loved me, and I don't feel so okay. I love Leah, and I'm pretty sure if things go on this way she won't be okay.*

So I did what I always do when I need information. I went to a bookstore. I found a couple of paperbacks on parenting—I don't even remember what they were, but they started my fascination with child development. (One book I found years later was actually titled *Loving Your Child is Not Enough.*)

Leah owes her mental health to this trip to the bookstore.

I consumed the books in a day. I craved them. They introduced me to the concept that parents can say something and children will hear it as something else. "That's not a nice thing to say" translates to, "You shouldn't feel that way." "Stop crying" might as well be, "Stop breathing," to a young child. It's as if there's a powerful code going on inside every word and sentence. I thought immediately of Mom's, "Who do you think you are?" She may have meant: "Don't push yourself so hard." But my daughter decoder heard: "Don't be a big shot."

I also expanded this notion of a code—of embedded meaning—to every human gesture of communication. I paid closer attention to Leah, and I realized I'd been force-feeding her. I think I was desperate to do the single life-sustaining act I knew—make sure she didn't starve. But in the process I'd been ignoring my baby's attempts to tell me she was full. We turned an important corner here.

Now when the crying spells hit, Leah and I slow-danced through Emmylou Harris or Van Morrison songs. She usually relaxed some, probably because I did. By the time she was six months old, the colic was over.

Leah said her first word before she was a year old. It was "juh," and by that she meant "juice." For a while, she built her vocabulary by using the beginning sound of every word. I joke that she started talking so young because she hadn't found any other way to get through to her mother. But by then, it really wasn't true. I adored being a mother, her mother. If she fell, I'd lift her, hug her onto my lap and soothe, "It'll be okay. It'll be okay," until she stopped crying. To this day the skin on my arms remembers the feeling of her sobs fading, then her head raising, looking to me for a way to move on. Sometimes I'd say, "This wouldn't happen if sidewalks were made of marshmallows." Or, "Shall we throw away that naughty table, or just scold it?" And she would wag her finger at the coffee table and laugh.

About that time, I found another book that became important to me: *Children: The Challenge*, by Rudolf Dreikurs. Re-reading it now, I find certain parts dated—gender stereotypes, for example. But Dreikurs guided me beyond Leah's infancy—when the single duty was her good care—to another, dawning duty: how to help her become a good person.

The book's principles are simple and, while they may not connect with all parents, they felt just right to me: You teach children competence by stepping back and letting them do whatever they can for themselves. You teach them right from wrong by letting them feel the "natural consequences"—as opposed to punishment—of anything they do wrong. Of course, you first have to be sure that the failing isn't your fault for expecting too much of them. Also, you do them the courtesy of trying to look at every circumstance from their point of view.

But my looking at the world with Leah's perspective became much more than a courtesy. It carried implicitly all the things I wanted her to feel from me—that I would always listen, that I cared, and that her feelings counted. Leah was eighteen months old when we moved to Florida. I remember one of our first trips to the beach, with a group of colleagues her father and I met at the newspaper. I have photos of Leah that day, her round baby shape still slightly suggestive of a duckling, a red plastic pail in her hands. We all expected her to love running into the lapping waves, but instead she backed away. I asked her, "So, what do you think of the ocean?" She looked up to me and said, "It's loud." I knelt, listened, and realized that at her level it certainly was. "You know, you're right," I said.

I also have clear memories of two times when I applied the natural-consequences lesson. Both happened when Leah was two. Once, at the grocery store, she was headed into a tantrum. I told her I needed her to be quiet until we got home, but the tantrum continued to build. She looked stunned when I picked her up from the grocery cart and told her, "This was a bad time to go shopping. You're so tired. We'll come back when you're rested." And we left the store. The second time, at a birthday party, Leah kept taking her friend's Barbie doll away from her. I told Leah we would have to leave if she didn't stop. She didn't, and we did go home. As I write about this now, I think I'm making it sound too easy. It's so tempting to let such little transgressions pass, and so hard to hurt the feelings of your precious child.

Then, about a year later, it all seemed worth it. My sister Trisch overheard Leah and a friend exploring Trisch's closet. Leah's friend wanted to play with her shoes. Leah said, "We should ask Aunt Trisch first." Her friend said, "She'll never know." And Leah said, "No, we should ask first." She had already internalized some sense of right and wrong. I was so proud of her.

We were in Fort Myers, Florida, for about three years. This was Leah's flamboyant period for clothing. It's when she decided she was partial to the clothes her Grandma Rosemarie sent her, "because they have pictures all over them." One day we went shopping for shoes, and she got a pair of flip-flops and canvas Mary Janes. She decided it wouldn't be "fair" to wear one and not the other, so until they wore out she wore a flip-flop on one foot and a Mary Jane on the other. I remember her wardrobe selection one night when we went to a friend's for dinner: a yellow tank top, a necklace of mismatched and multicolored beads, blue-and-pink floral pajama bottoms and tiny work boots on her feet.

She looked in the mirror and felt beautiful.

These will always be precious years for me. I worked part time, and loved my days with Leah. We swam so much that the Florida sun and pool chlorine bleached Leah's hair blond. Zen Buddhism talks of seeing life with a "beginner's mind," and anybody who has spent time with a two- or three-year-old child knows exactly what that means. Everything is fascinating. A trip to the grocery store is like going to the circus. Even loading a washing machine, piece by soiled piece, is an adventure. And then, when you take the clothes out, they're wet!

I loved reading to Leah. I discovered the children's classics—Winnie-the-Pooh, Peter Pan—with her. I don't think Mom read them to us. I probably wouldn't have sat still for them. And how was she to know of the traditional English-language books? I'll never forget the day Leah's brain made the connection between the ABC jingle and the capacity for assembled letters to carry meaning. I saw a "shazam" moment on her face—she was four or five. The magic trigger: A.A. Milne.

Sometimes she was scary smart. When Leah was twenty-two months old, her baby-sitter must have started talking to her about toilet training. One day, she lay face up on her bed while I changed her diaper. And referring to two of my newspaper colleagues—both of whom Leah knew—she asked me, "Does Jan Godown poop in her pants?" I paused because I had no idea where she was going with this. I answered, "No, she doesn't." Then she asked, "Does Bob Morris poop in his pants?" And I told her that he didn't. She looked thoughtful. Within a few weeks, she had practically toilet trained herself.

One morning, shortly before Leah started kindergarten, she told me a dream she'd had. It's probably oedipal, but I like to think it's also a sign of security. She said, "A man came in at night and said he was going to kill me. So I told him, 'My mom's in the other room. You can kill her instead.'" I thought: *That's how a child should feel, certain that her mother would take a bullet for her.*

She started to enjoy making up her own stories, so I wrote them down and we assembled some of them into a booklet for Christmas gifts that year.

One was "Super Leah:"

Hi. I'm Wonder Woman. W-o-o-o, I'm so tired, fighting crime all day, you know. You wouldn't believe how much crime there is. And I only get one day off a year. And what I really want to do is get married to Steve. He doesn't want to marry me because he's not a Superhero. But what the heck? I wasn't a Superhero when I married Superman.

'Course, I understand, because I felt the same way when I married Superman. I just spent three days running fast ... and pushing heavy things ... and getting strong so I could be a Superhero, too. Cuz I can't cry or be hurt. I always have to be strong.

My daughter keeps wanting to put on my Super-clothes, but I tell her, "No, you're too young." She's only four. My son keeps wanting to put on Superman's suit, too, but Superman says he's too small. 'Course, with his suit, one size fits all so I don't know why he says that. The End.

We recorded her first chicken joke:

Why did the chicken cross the ocean? To get to New Jersey, because the chicken was in Africa.

We recorded her first prayer:

Thank you for the food we eat. I hope you are at my command. Grace.

And we recorded her first take on religion:

I don't believe in God. What is there for him to do? Factories make plastic, and people keep each other warm.

Over the years, some of the hardest times for Leah were our frequent moves to take job promotions. She left friends and a preschool she loved when we moved from Florida to

Rochester, New York. She left her kindergarten class and all her friends when we moved from there to Omaha, Nebraska. The hardest move was from there to Long Island, New York, when Leah was in fifth grade. It meant leaving her friends, her school and much of her family. I feel like I let her down this time. I tried to help her with her new classes. I made her bedroom—a girl's oasis—a priority in fixing up our new house. But I also started working long hours, so when she needed more of me I wasn't there. I broke my own rule—don't expect too much of a child—and Leah rose to the occasion. It's hard to find your way into groups of girlfriends at that age. But Leah made nice friends. She never let her grades drop. I know I remained an important source of security for her, but I also know she felt cracks in that foundation.

One story from those years shows what I mean. At sixteen she wanted to look for a job. I told her a strategy I'd seen in a newspaper story. We wrote up a teenage version of a resume: Leah's school awards, her baby-sitting as work experience, references from teachers. We mailed it to law firms in the area, because Leah thought she might like to be a lawyer one day. At a time when laid-off Grumman engineers were working at burger chains, Leah got job offers to be an office clerk from two law firms. I gave myself a big pat on the back: What a great experience for her. What a success. Only years later did I learn that one of the firms called her late one afternoon and told her she needed to come in immediately if she wanted a job interview. Her father and I were at work, so Leah assumed the responsibility for getting herself there. It was raining, so she couldn't walk. I think she finally got a ride with a friend of a friend. I believe teenagers should assume they can call their parents for help at a time like this. No sixteen-year-old should have to feel that self-reliant, but Leah did.

That episode reminds me of a book that my therapist, Judy, gave me to read: *The Drama of the Gifted Child*, by Alice Miller. The book is about the legacy of distant, critical parents. Their children tend to grow up endlessly trying to figure out how to please their parents—so much so that as adults they have trouble figuring out what they want and who they are, apart from their parents' wishes. They also become extreme perfectionists. In my own therapy, I saw a lot of myself in the title role of the book. But now when I read it, I see my mother, crushed by her father's anger. And, more painfully, I see my daughter, too. Like the gifted children in the book, Leah expects way too much of herself.

Through the years, my relationship with my parents was sometimes good, sometimes middling, and often a little hostile under the surface. It felt to me like they bit hard into certain themes and just kept chewing on them. Mom always made fun of my use of parenting books. "No book can tell you about your child," she scoffed. At those times, I heard defensive words come out of my mouth, when what I wanted to say was, "I know that, Mom. And I know I'm making all kinds of mistakes as a mother. But I wish you would tell me that you're proud of how hard I'm trying." As for Dad, for some reason he grew virulently anti-education. He could still swing a punch. "The more people go to school, the stupider they get," he often said to me. When I lived in Omaha, and I got an M.A. in English literature at Creighton University, my parents refused to come to my graduation—even though they lived only eighty miles away. My in-laws came—driving twice the distance—but my parents did not.

I think all that has something to do with why I experienced our parents somewhat differently from the way my sisters did. Something about me seemed to set them off. I liked school and learning—which made me a geek in my eyes, but somewhere inside Mom I think I was a big, bad echo of her father. I liked my work—and even though my career had some serious ups and downs, it must have ignited bitter memories inside Dad of his mother, whose preoccupation with success and social standing always made him feel like a failure. "Like he always said, his mother's friends had 'positions' and he had a 'job,'" Mom told me.

It's amazing to me ... all this stuff that goes on invisibly and yet so powerfully. After Mom died, I wanted to find out more about the silent influences she and I had brought to our relationship.

My journey started in Minnesota where I found a particularly relevant branch of family research: the science of mother-child attachment. I had a passing acquaintance with it from a college science course years ago. I'd heard of the baby monkeys who had only wire "mothers" with bottles, and who grew stunted or died young—even though they didn't lack for food. I learned that the simple act of covering the wire with fur was enough to let the baby monkeys bond to this "mother," and fare much better. And I knew that the new and most startling lesson of all was that mother's touch can matter as much as mother's milk.

A lot of research on mother-child attachment is going on at the University of Minnesota in Minneapolis. One study there has followed a group of families for thirty years, and the force of this bond tracked over time astounds me.

Mothers are mostly unaware of their particular style of attachment. It is instinctive, not deliberate—usually a copy of how they were mothered. The great power of those earliest exchanges comes from the monopoly that mothers hold on their babies' access to the world. They are a baby's connection to all life beyond their soft skin.

When attachment works as it should—and it usually does—there is a baby who cries out for the necessities of life and a mother who hears and makes everything all right again. A "hungry" cry is rewarded with food. A "cold" cry brings a blanket. This baby feels safe, and over time even begins to feel like a person of influence. The implicit lesson the baby learns is: "I have the power to make happy endings." This baby comes to believe that the world is an okay place and that based on a sample of one—Mother—people are a nice part of it.

That becomes reality for the baby and the template for all future relationships. In research terms that means more self-confident, less hostile, better at negotiating disagreements. In life that means getting along well with people—on the playground, in school, in work, in marriage, in book clubs and in bowling leagues.

About a year into life, the baby's "job" changes from finding security to exploring the world. This adds a new duty to the mother's job description: She becomes the safe zone that her baby steps out of in bold moments and runs back to when tired or afraid. She is warm and welcoming. But she also encourages her little adventurer to wander, and celebrates the pride and confidence that grow with every new step.

In some families, the attachment process doesn't go as it should. The most disastrous is a variation called "disorganized" attachment. This can happen with an abusive mother, for example. Now a baby's safe zone is also the danger zone, a hopeless state of affairs. All this baby knows is confusion and fear and conflict. One of the saddest things

I heard in attachment research was the story of a baby in this circumstance who would be seen backing away from his mother. This baby couldn't take his eyes off the primal, instinctive object of security that he so desperately wanted to be near. But he backed away from her—put some distance between them—because he never knew if she would hug him or hit him. Just imagine the disturbing way that baby's neurons are firing, and all that portends for ten or twenty years later.

Another variation in mother-child attachments is "anxious-resistant." Mothers in these relationships are unpredictable, sometimes responding to a baby's cry but other times not. This trains babies to carry on and on, because the odds are she'll have to come one of these times. I picture these babies growing into the children we all see at grocery checkout lines: They want the candy bar in the rack. Mom says no. They ask again. Mom says no again. Then, as the volume builds, Mom gives in and the child gets the chocolate.

The third variation was what, I believe, my mother and I had: "anxious-avoidant" attachment.

Mothers in these relationships consistently—you might say, reliably—ignore their babies' cries. These mothers dislike fussing babies, often seeing them as difficult, unnecessarily demanding. Their babies pick up on this and—contrary to the screamers in variation #2—they learn to be quiet, to not look too needy or too emotional. They learn to maneuver themselves only as close to their mothers as they're allowed. I picture them like forest animals drawn to a campfire, ringing around its warmth but easily frightened away by alarmed campers. These children learn a certain reserve. Their parents often boast about how independent, how self-reliant they are.

My poison-apple dream is the story of an anxious-avoidant child. An adult came, cast me away, and I blamed myself for being suckered by an apple.

Many things can make a mother like this. One is the popular old notion that picking up crying babies will spoil them. Another is a life that has trained a woman to be deaf to emotions—starting all the way back to her own. And my mother had that life in spades.

A tyrant father. A world war. An alcoholic husband. As she said, survival for her meant not stopping for feelings. Germans who talked in *Kriegskinder* of their childhoods during World War II kept repeating my mother's theme: Feelings are worse than futile, they are self-indulgent.

It's no surprise, then, that attachment research also goes on in Germany. I went to meet Klaus and Karin Grossmann, near Munich, who did the first major attachment work there in the 1970s. I'd heard general accounts that gave me the impression the Grossmanns had studied the attachments between women my mother's age and their children, and their research found the highest rate of anxious-avoidant attachment of any study in the world up to that time—49 percent. Twenty percent is more typical.

I got a shock when I read more about the Grossmanns' research in several German academic journals. It turns out their subjects in fact were women who had babies in 1976. That meant precisely me. That put me and not my mother in their 49-percent category. And sure enough, as I considered this new twist, I could see the evidence that I fit the type. Force-feeding is a big sign, because these mothers often are very responsible and want to take good care of their babies. They just don't know how. The other sign was Leah's hyper maturity, her hyper sense of self-reliance. So it turns out that I am my mother's daughter.

There was one more surprise in the Grossmanns' study. By the time the children in the anxious-avoidant group reached age sixteen, they were indistinguishable from the securely attached group.

What was going on? The Grossmanns speculate that cultural differences may be at play. The results varied so much, showing up-and-down swings over the years of research that followed in Germany. It could be that the research technique, developed with heavy Canadian and English influences, simply does not fit Germans. As adults, these children did have above-average partner problems. But their overall ability to form close relationships was substantial. And one explanation for that could be that while these mothers were not as warm and fuzzy with their babies, they were so good at the exploration phase— supportive and proud—that they formed their strong and close attachments then.

I also wonder if my German equivalents had handled motherhood the way I had: We started with the insecure legacy of our mothers and then took some time to reprogram ourselves. We could. Unlike our mothers, we didn't have to spend our days stooping into bomb shelters and worrying about our next meals. All of my reading and ruminating were without doubt a privilege of my time and place. My journey back to World War II makes me clear on that. So does the USS Cole. So does Fallujah.

I think that what happened to us is exactly what Minnesota researchers found happened in a study of mothers who had been abused as children. Those who broke the cycle of cruelty did so consciously. They were more likely to have had psychotherapy. And if not, they found another way to come to terms with their childhoods. The critical point was not what happened to them. The mothers who fared the best had the clearest memories. They didn't try to forget or deny the treatment they had endured. They kept no dark secrets. They figured out some kind of acceptance.

The researchers see this as absolutely great news. It's not possible to turn back time and give people new childhoods.

But it seems to be possible to heal them in the here and now.

I suppose what therapy gave me was a way to look at life from Mom's perspective, something like Leah and the ocean. There's a place on the tapes of her talking about her life where I asked her how she felt when she learned her fiancé was dead.

"I wasn't ever an emotional cripple that I know," she told me.

"Well, I don't think you'd have to be an emotional cripple to be upset about that," I said.

"Don't pull that psychology on me," she said. "I don't have any idea how I felt. Nobody ever asked me how I felt about anything."

I took her comments to mean that she considered me an emotional cripple for dwelling on such things. I spent a lot of years feeling hurt, accused of weakness after similar conversations. It took me a long time to realize that my questions left Mom feeling accused, too. I had to learn to listen to her tell her story as she lived it. And I had to learn to hear all the ways she expressed love—no hugs but beautifully knit sweaters, Saturday morning phone calls, and always saying exactly what was on her mind. For every time I was disappointed that she couldn't be happy for me, there was an unhappy time—my divorce, my illness—when I felt her solid support. And her body gave the lie to her toughness.

When she was worried about one of her daughters, her migraines would come back, or her psoriasis would flare, or her digestion would go haywire.

There is so much to love and admire about my mother—her courage, her humor, her intelligence, and the great responsibilities she shouldered for my sisters and me. I am glad I am her daughter, and I am glad she knew that.

My daughter and I, on the other hand, live in a world of emotions. Leah has felt my embrace—truly and later figuratively—throughout her life. When we moved to Long Island, it looked like she needed to catch up on a few math lessons, so I studied with her every night. When she pushed herself so hard through high school—she is her mother's daughter, too—I figured out that Thursdays were her regular meltdown nights, so we tried to order pizza or get ice cream or do something to preemptively lighten the mood. When I picked her up from college after her freshman year, we talked nonstop through the eight-hour drive home. "I didn't think we'd talk the whole time," I told her. "Really?" she asked, surprised I could imagine otherwise. When, in college, Leah met the man who would become her husband, she called and asked me to come see him. I was touched that she cared so much about my opinion. And when she told me of sitting at the Minneapolis airport waiting to fly back to graduate school—and wondering how the world could just go on as if her mother wasn't seriously ill in the hospital—she knew I'd understand how scared she was.

There is so much to love and admire about my daughter—her courage, her humor, her intelligence, and the great feelings she has for people. I am glad I am her mother, and I am glad she knows that.

~:Epilogue:~

By Leah Stanton, daughter of H.J. Cummins

My mother and I have talked many times through the years about my grandmother Rose. Sometimes about the tremendous trials she must have experienced early in her life (we were often guessing; Rose usually did not want to talk about it). Sometimes we talked about her personality—her toughness, fortitude, and, in many ways, her emotional distance. For example, I called her Rose, not Grandma Rose, the way my cousins usually did.

We have also talked about our relationship as mother and daughter. I think we have both always treasured our relationship (except, of course, for a few years in adolescence when I thought my mom one of the most embarrassing people on the planet). So, when my mother decided to write this book, she asked if I would write a little bit about my experiences and feelings.

Rose

When I first began thinking about my relationship with Rose, I kept thinking that she scared me. Now, in reflecting on this, "scared" is not completely accurate. I would describe my feeling as "intimidated." But, as a child, I was scared. I truly believe that Rose loved me, but I just never felt like she knew what to do with me. Even though she had raised three daughters, I felt like kids were a bit of a mystery to her. This was in sharp contrast to my paternal grandmother, who rigged up her entire basement as a playhouse for me, and always remembered my favorite foods.

As an adult and a licensed social worker, I have more understanding of what, I guess, was Rose's parenting style. Her life was such that grit, tenacity, and plain old toughness were essential for survival. Maybe she tried to pass that on to her children, and her grandchildren. It always felt like a mismatch, though, with my life experience. I never had to worry about my physical safety, about finding food, about avoiding true danger. I wanted hugs, jokes, and plenty of warm cookies.

I can't remember any real conversations with Rose, any heart-to-hearts about life, what I wanted or was hoping for, if I had a boyfriend, and so on. Mostly what I remember was hanging out in her living room, with Rose sitting in her recliner, smoking. I still think of her whenever I hear a smoker's cough, or raspy, bronchial breathing. And I remember the smell of stale tobacco that would rise up when I would open a package mailed from her. I guess when I think about my relationship with Rose, I think of a relationship missed, a relationship largely undeveloped, unexplored.

Mom

This is in sharp contrast to my relationship with my mother. Every day of my life I have felt confident in her love for me, and her genuine delight in being a mom. This is not to say that our relationship has always been easy. She took parenting very seriously, sometimes, I think, to the detriment of plain, old-fashioned fun.

I think about Mom's approach to parenting as akin to learning a foreign language. When you are first learning any second language, you cling to the rules of grammar, syntax, and pronunciation, because without them you quickly lose your hold on any useful communication. This is so different from the experience of those who are raised in a bilingual household. Here, the language seeps into them almost effortlessly, and their comfort and ease with speaking it is present from the beginning. They just don't have to focus so hard on the basics, and can play with idioms and unique expressions in a way that a beginning language scholar simply cannot.

I think of Mom as that beginning language scholar. She didn't learn a lot, or perhaps just not things she was comfortable with repeating, from her mother. She didn't grow up with the language of motherhood. So she set out to learn it herself. I think I was raised, quite literally, "by the book," whatever the parenting book was of the time.

This wasn't always easy for me. As a young child, there were many rules to follow—proper bedtimes, educational activities, strict behavioral expectations. I had an allotted amount of television viewing time, I wrote book reports on my personal reading, and I thought granola bars were candy bars until sometime in kindergarten. I was a born people-pleaser, so I took my mother's expectations to heart. As I grew older, I think we both relaxed a little more, and didn't have to try quite so hard to be a "good" mother and daughter.

Despite these examples, the constant of my childhood is my mother's love. I have always felt that she loved me, as my own person, and really sought to know who I was. What a blessing to be known like that, not just as a reflection of someone else, but as yourself. What a rarity. I adore my mother. I respect her. And I feel so safe in our relationship—the tremendous effort she put into parenting me when I was three is still there as I approach thirty.

Me

I am expecting my first child in a few months. Consequently, I have been thinking about parenting a lot lately: What kind of parent do I want to be? How can I balance letting

my children be whoever they are with my role as a social-
izing agent into the larger world? What if I'm too selfish to
be a good mother?

Perhaps this is when I feel most blessed for my mother.
She had to learn the new language; I was raised with the
language of motherhood. This is not to diminish the tremendous challenges that I will inevitably face. However, I
feel like I am starting with the grammar, syntax, and vocabulary. How fortunate that I can build on that foundation, and hopefully embrace the playfulness and ease that
can come from it.

Every relationship is a work in progress. I suppose the
best you can hope for is that those you are in relationship
with care enough to stretch and grow, and invest energy and
effort. I'm not sure if my mom had that with Rose. I know I
have that with my mother. I hope for that with my child.

∽: Sources :∽

Byron Egeland and Martha Farrell Erickson. "Findings from the Parent-Child Project and Implications for Early Intervention." *Zero to Three* 20:2 (October/November 1999).
This article is an easy-to-understand introduction to the attachment research at the University of Minnesota.

L. Alan Sroufe, Byron Egeland, Elizabeth A. Carlson, W. Andrew Collins. *The Development of the Person: The Minnesota Study of Risk and Adaptation From Birth to Adulthood.* New York: The Guilford Press, 2005.
The book reviews three decades of research at the University of Minnesota that tracked 180 children and their families. The authors address the inevitable questions: As people grow and mature, how powerful is early attachment and where do life experiences fit in?

Martha Farrell Erickson, Karen Kurz-Riemer. *Infants, Toddlers and Families: A Framework for Support and Intervention.* New York: The Guilford Press, 1999.
The book, a guide to professionals who work with children and families, is also a user-friendly look at attachment research.

Rauh, H. (2000): Bindungsforschung im deutschsprachigen Raum; Einführung in das Themen-Doppelheft. Psychologie in Erziehung und Unterricht, 2000, 47, 81-86. (Hellgard Rauh, Universität Potsdam).
Gloger-Tippelt, G., Vetter, J., Rauh, H. (2000). Untersuchungen mit der "Fremden Situation" in deutschsprachigen Ländern: Ein Überblick. Psychologie in Erziehung und Unterricht, 2000, 47, 87-98.
Both are articles in an edition of the German journal, "Psychologie in Erziehung und Unterricht" (Psychology of Development and Learning). They are a collection and comparison of fifteen attachment studies in German-speaking countries from 1977 to 1995.

Lorenz, Hilke. *Kriegskinder: Das Schicksal Einer Generation* [Children of War: The Fate of One Generation]. Munich: List Publisher, 2003.
This book, written in German, is a collection of the memories of dozens of Germans who were children during World War II.